D0192744

Landscapes of
Aging and Spirituality

Landscapes of Aging and Spirituality

ESSAYS

Kathleen Montgomery, Editor

Skinner House Books
Boston

Copyright © 2015 by the Unitarian Universalist Association. All rights reserved. Published by Skinner House Books, an imprint of the Unitarian Universalist Association, a liberal religious organization with more than 1,000 congregations in the U.S. and Canada, 24 Farnsworth St., Boston, MA 02210–1409.

www.skinnerhouse.org

Printed in the United States

Cover and text design by Suzanne Morgan

Photo of Kathleen Montgomery by Adrien Bisson, www.adrienbisson.com

print ISBN: 978-1-55896-759-5
eBook ISBN: 978-1-55896-760-1

6 5 4 3
17 16 15

Library of Congress Cataloging-in-Publication Data
Landscapes of aging and spirituality : essays / Kathleen Montgomery, editor.

    pages cm
 ISBN 978-1-55896-759-5 (pbk. : alk. paper)—ISBN 978-1-55896-760-1 (ebook) 1. Older people--Religious life. 2. Aging—Religious aspects—Unitarian Universalist churches. I. Montgomery, Kathleen (Kathleen C.), editor.
 BL625.4.S94 2015
 242ʾ.65—dc23

2014044941

This book is dedicated to my grandchildren—

Cameron, Ian, Simon, Skyler,
Summer, and James—

with the hope that many years from now
they too will find companionship here.

—KM

That was fast.
I mean life.

—RON PADGETT

Contents

Preface   xi

The Buddha in My Bedroom   1
  Jane Ranney Rzepka

Like Potato Chips   7
  Tom Schade

A Person of a Certain Age   11
  Patricia Tummino

A Witness to Life, Death, and Then   19
  Carl Scovel

Beginner's Mind   27
  Maureen Killoran

Rise in Body or in Spirit   33
  William Sinkford

A Woman of Worth   47
  Lynn Thomas Strauss

Memento Mori   55
  Burton D. Carley

On Turning Seventy   65
   Phyllis B. O'Connell

For Most This Amazing Life   73
   Richard S. Gilbert

Being Still   83
   Judith Meyer

Possessed   87
   Peter Morales

Recently Retired   93
   Kate Tucker

Lesson from Great Pond   103
   Gary E. Smith

The Small Stuff   109
   Denise Taft Davidoff

A Song in the Face of Death   115
   John Cummins

Exit Strategies   121
   Susan Weston

Time Travel   131
   Martin Teitel

The Path   139
   Mark Belletini

About the Contributors   149

Preface

On the table by my bed I keep a photograph of my maternal grandmother. She was both my mother's and my father's favorite person. I grew up hearing stories of her. In the photo, taken probably at the turn of the last century, she wears a pleated, high-necked dress and a wide-brimmed hat with a huge fabric flower on it; she's handsome and strong looking. She was a successful businesswoman, one of the first women in Detroit to drive a car, and, after a brief marriage, the single parent of three children, all of whom loved her unreservedly.

I never knew that grandmother. She died of influenza in 1927, well before I was born. But I realized in my forties that I had been taught to model myself after her, to live up to her standard—loving and intrepid. I've failed, of course, but for years I consulted with her, or at least with my imagination of her, whenever I felt lost, looking for guidance and wisdom about my decisions.

When my grandmother died she was much younger than I am now. So even in my fertile imagination, consulting with her about aging seems unrealistic. As I've entered my seventies, retired, begun to acknowledge changes in my body, tried to figure out how to "be" in well-past-middle age, watched friends die, and thought a great deal about my spiritual life, I've wanted—not advice, really—but companionship for this latter-part-of-life journey.

This collection is the result of that yearning. I went to some of the people who I thought might fill that role for me and asked them to write, with as much self-revelation as they felt comfortable, about their experience of aging and how that experience intersected with their spiritual lives and their sense of meaning. Some were close friends, some I barely knew, some I knew only second-hand. The results far exceeded my expectations. Astonished me, really.

The writers range in age from mid-sixties to late-eighties, all middle class, all have had satisfying careers, all are Unitarian Universalists. Hardly diverse. And yet their experiences seem universal. In each one I've found some part of myself, the joyful parts and the tough and tender parts. I trust others will too.

I am deeply grateful to each of these essayists who have chosen to bare a bit of their interior life. They each describe the landscape of their life as they see it now—the memories, regrets, satisfactions, losses, pleasures. It's the stuff of all of life but perhaps a bit more poignant and keenly felt as the horizon nears.

The French have a phrase for that part of the day when it is no longer daylight but not yet dark, *L'Heure Bleue*. In English, The Blue Hour. Photographers call it "the sweet hour" because of the quality of the light. That's how I've come to think of this stage of life: bittersweet and beautiful because of the quality of the remaining light.

—Kathleen Montgomery

The Buddha in My Bedroom

JANE RANNEY RZEPKA

The statue on my bureau is about four feet long and maybe a foot tall. All white. A reclining Buddha. I bought him because he lies there radiating serenity in spite of his situation, whatever it is. I am not a Buddhist, but that's how he looks to me. When the postpolio symptoms began to lay me low, I thought he would be just the ticket. And he is.

According to Buddhist sources, the reclining Buddha is sleeping, resting, enlightened, or dead. Because for the rest of time I will be doing a lot of sleeping, resting, or being dead (enlightenment is out of the question), I feel comforted by this statue. His message is not "Keep busy." It's not "You can still be productive." And it's certainly not "Get out, kick up your heels, and dance the fandango." Or whatever. He's okay with being on death's door, and I like seeing that when I wake up in the morning.

Of course, I'm not on death's door, as far as I know, but that's the direction we're all heading as the birthdays accumulate. And as they do, we're going to have to take it down a notch.

Myself, I'm aging precociously and no longer in fine fettle, so there's a lot I won't be doing. Mine is a reverse bucket list. Skiing. At least not real skiing like in the old days: fast, aggressive, daring. Maybe on some scarcely discernible incline with my granddaughter, who's three. And I won't be trekking anymore with a big heavy backpack. Dainty walks are more like it. My bike is gathering dust, and rust. The artist Paul Klee said that people are "half winged—half imprisoned," and the balance is shifting for me.

Professionally, in the eyes of the world, no doubt I've preached enough sermons, attended enough meetings, taught enough classes, written enough words, worked enough for social justice, done enough ministry over the past forty years. I understand. "Move aside, Jane, it's not your turn anymore." As I'm a lifelong friend of anonymity, really, moving to the background is not too hard. Sure, I feel the occasional pang, but I am almost always delighted by the recently ordained, and pleased to hand the whole thing over. Know when to hold 'em, know when to fold 'em.

2

The fact is, the world replenishes. Out with the old, in with the new. Whoever said "one hundred years, all new people" was spot on, and, for me, it's an observation to celebrate. New brainpower, fresh enthusiasm, novel ways of knowing, and, I hope, better ways of treating one another. As the clock ticks down, I'll miss the people who watched with wonder the first airplanes flying overhead, or learned Latin and Greek as a matter of course, or herded cattle on horses, or remember their grandmother's corsets. And then, a few years later, I'll miss the folks who lived through World War II, the dawn of television, and eventually the invention of the hula hoop and instant mashed potatoes. I'd draw the line here, if I could. But finally it will be me—who remembers mumps, life before cell phones, ATMs, and the Pill—who's being replaced.

It turns out that I celebrate this Ultimate Replenishment only in theory. The Buddha in my bedroom would not be pleased. The truth is, I can feel a touch of panic in the outskirts of my consciousness. Not about dying but about running out of time. Running out of time and feeling increasingly greedy for life. I like the way the accretions of memories, loves, ponderings, and various goings-on have created a sense of self for me, a

3

consistent and reliable companion over the years, and I feel an animal passion for keeping it going. I still look forward.

For starters, I want to continue to wallow— more being than doing—in a big sphere. To float in a river that's very far away and an odd color of blue, crazy birds squawking overhead. How about that? And crawl around in my garden enough to develop a deep knowledge of its ways. And love all the family and all the friends that will have me. I would love to sit in the desert with people who speak tribal languages I can't identify. Have you noticed how much music there is, and how many books? And how compelling silence is? In addition, let me just say that I have 119 movies in my Netflix queue. Greedy for life.

Naturally, this world includes things I don't like, never have, and would appreciate a future without. Most of them go without saying: injustice, killing, suffering, tragedy of all kinds. These are things we can work on, and we will. But there are trivial things not to like, and now that I'm old, I have allowed myself to name them, if not avoid them altogether: blue cheese, prickers, the hokey-pokey, sleet, sing-alongs, pratfalls. These I am not going to work on. To hell with them.

But the main feature of the future, my future, that is—the one with decreasing functional hours—is all the life-giving connections. How can I contain them all? A favorite spot on the ocean, year after year after year, where the babies toddled and friendships deepened and suddenly the babies have their own babies and the grownups are gray and stiff as we navigate the rocks. An astoundingly congenial family of brothers and sisters and their partners and kids. Colleagues, now friends, who have known one another since we were baby ministers, and a religion that has sustained and inspired me for all my life. At the center of it all—my life, I mean—is my own little family, growing now with daughters-in-law and grandchildren, such deep connections that I have no words for it.

And here's an image. My husband and I were married when we were twenty years old, so we've had time to get attached. Lately, when I was in the midst of a tough cancer procedure, I tried to do what you're supposed to—imagine a peaceful place, make use of relaxation techniques, listen to soothing music, that sort of thing. I ran through the list, but nothing helped. Finally, I conjured up my husband's hand resting lightly on my back. That's what worked.

The connections pile up, egged on by the gratitude and the memories that themselves have piled up. And though the moths have gotten at the memories, and they're full of holes, I know where I've come from. The places I've lived and loved, the people who surrounded me—the characters, the relatives, the best friends—the beliefs that sustained me, the ideas that fired me up, they're all welcome tethers.

All this connection in the face of letting go leaves me in a bit of a pickle. A paradox: Committed to the mandatory process of detaching, I grow more attached to living, the reclining Buddha in my bedroom notwithstanding. Eventually, the problem will take care of itself, of course, no matter how much I love life. I will let go, be gone, and that will be that.

Overall, to be frank, I find aging, not to mention death, a preposterous state of affairs. And meaningless. Not at all the way I would have set it up. Sorry—I do hate to say that out loud because no one likes to hear it—but you asked, and an indifferent universe has always been a part of my theology. I'm not angry about it or especially sad—that's just the way it works.

Indeed, my friends, in spite of the prospect of aging and death, for now, inexplicably, I feel happy. And grateful. I always have, and with any luck at all, I always will.

Like Potato Chips

TOM SCHADE

A wise man in a congregation I served once said that we should not make a bucket list—that list of everything we want to do before we kick the bucket. I had to listen, because he was an inspirational leader in the congregation, a distinguished physician, and a widely respected leader in our city.

He had also been living with more than one form of cancer, one of which, ironically, was in his very field of medical specialization. He had been given up for dead more than once. He first visited our church while searching for a place to have his memorial service. But there he was, up in the pulpit, big as life and radiating hope.

"No bucket list," he preached. He had concluded that when you crossed off that last item—the skydiving adventure, that trip to Bali—you would be giving yourself permission to die. And so you would.

He spoke as if the fuels of life were desire and anticipation. As if to keep living you need something still undone, some unmet goal. The secret to a long and happy life is to keep moving the goalposts farther away, to keep yearning for new adventures. When I have finally seen Paris, I should then set my sights on Rio or Capetown or even Vienna, Ohio, my old hometown.

I reflected on this wisdom. And I have found I have gone the other way. It occurs to me that I have met by now all the greatest goals of my life, and I am just sixty-four.

I have participated in the great stories of my time. I picketed; I marched; I argued loudly with comrades and compatriots; I leafleted factory gates at dawn and worked on a presidential campaign. I did my soul searching and privilege checking, lost and made friends over great causes. I've been right and I've been wrong. Was I ever at the center? No, I never needed to be, but I did not let my times go by.

I have loved someone wise and strong and kind, and that someone has loved me, and we have been together for more than half my life.

I have fathered two children; they are wise, strong, and kind women. I have watched them form families of their own with their own wise, strong, and kind partners.

I have been loved by a beautiful little grandchild, and I have been promised more to come. I share my home with two charming little dogs, whose devotion to me seems unlimited. On the other hand, some magnificent and majestic cats have permitted me to serve them food and to clean their litter box and even, on occasion, to pet them. What more could anyone ask?

I have served an exemplary Unitarian Universalist church as their minister and have received the respect of my colleagues. I have fulfilled my professional ambitions.

So, if I have been working all my life on my bucket list, I can cross off all the important goals. Yes, there is much I still want, many experiences that I would love to have. But they would be *more*. And more is not the same as happier.

My daughters tell me not to expect any more than five or six grandchildren. But if I had ten grandchildren, I would still want another. And if I became deathly ill, I would hang on long enough to see number eleven come to my bedside. But number eleven could not make me any happier than I am right now.

I will always want more time with my wife and more time with my daughters, especially if we could spend that time in Rio or Barcelona or Capetown. And even if that extra time is in a hospital bed in the living room, it will not make me any happier than I already am.

I know that I will leave the great cause of justice unfinished, no matter what is accomplished in my lifetime. I have found my joy, as the poet Marge Piercy writes, in going "into the fields to harvest and work in a row and pass the bags along." Happy is not the same as satisfied.

The good things in life are like potato chips: delicious, but never quite satisfying; you always want more. But more is not the same as happier.

I suppose I have unthinkingly made my own sort of bucket list. I feel good about it because I have put up top all that I have done already: the work that has made me proud, the love given and received, the people and animals with whom I have shared my life. I can cross them off now and stop grasping so desperately at life.

This may be only the golden afternoon of a long, long day. But for this moment, I feel at peace with my mortality.

A Person of a Certain Age

PATRICIA TUMMINO

I began switching my sons' names in my fifties. I have a hard time keeping track of my calendar. And now that I'm sixty-five, don't ask for any detail about the movie I saw last week. I am pleased to report that I have always had excellent memory for music (although I have no musical gifts—this is God's way of teasing me) but, alas, I have a lousy memory for faces and voices. People commonly say, "I may forget names but I never forget a face." That's not me. I am capable of forgetting every-thing. This doesn't feel okay.

I was concerned enough to bring my poor memory to my doctor's attention, and he referred me to a neurologist, who arranged for a battery of physical and neurological tests. The neurologist, Dr. D., said that my memory is well within the range of normal for "a woman of your age." Women who have serious trouble, he said, are unaware of how their memory loss affects others and are usually brought in by concerned family members. He sent me home with a statin for high cholesterol and multivitamins.

Dr. D. did mention one variable that could skew the results a bit. Intelligence can mask a poor memory. I occasionally think about that one, trying to decide which story line I prefer for myself. Would I rather think of myself as healthy and average for a woman of my age? Or intelligent and dealing with memory loss at a threshold currently too low to show up in testing? This is the first time I have ever worried that smart might be a problem.

The other thing that festered a bit in what Dr. D. said was his use of the phrase *a woman of your age*. This feels like code for a diminution of what is expected of me because of my age, and my first baby step toward the invisibility that comes with being truly old. I was tempted to hunt down my baby book, were it still extant, and enter, toward the back, way after "Baby's First Step," the date on which I was first called *a woman of your age*. A bittersweet accomplishment.

If reaching a level of decline where you're called *a woman of your age* were to be considered an accomplishment, it is a standard that, so far, my mother-in-law, who lives with us, has failed. At eighty-nine, she can tell you what she had for breakfast every day last week and I'm sure she can easily name everyone she's met since moving in with us two years ago. She is also a voracious reader of mysteries and thrillers who can remember not only which James Patterson novels she's read but their plots and titles as well. As far as I'm concerned, that's savant territory.

Meanwhile, I have asked Dr. D. to explain what is going on with me, and his answer is, basically, that aging is going on. There are ways in which I have aged more quickly than my mother-in-law. That is humbling.

I confess that I have developed some compensatory behaviors, like a designated spot in the house for my car keys and pocketbook. The neighbors must wonder at times why my husband spends so much time in the driveway before we go out in the evening. They can't see that while he waits, I'm zipping around inside the house looking for my pocketbook. The teacher in me knows what to do—give important things assigned seats. My pocketbook now belongs on a shelf in the library and my keys are assigned to a hook in the kitchen.

13

This helps, whenever I can remember to use the hooks.

But I can't assign everything to a fixed location. I seem to move things around all day long. The cell phone, the laundry, the groceries, the car, personal items, books, sweaters, hats, mail, pens and pencils. All of it gets shuffled with use, most of it while I'm on autopilot. So nowadays I try to take an extra moment to stay alert long enough to note when I am putting something down. Autopilot is now my enemy.

And then there's the hearing loss. Most people who know me aren't aware that I am somewhat hard of hearing, mainly because no one needs to shout for me to hear them. Even so, I've developed some simple behaviors to cope with my mild hearing loss. When walking I try to keep my companions to my left to favor my good ear. And in a restaurant I try to sit in the middle of the table rather than at the end. Visiting the audiologist is now on my to-do list.

One bad habit I haven't yet broken myself of is my tendency to zone out when many voices are talking over one another. When casual listening becomes work, I'll smile and nod, looking as though I'm taking things in when I'm actually thinking about that to-do list and wondering if I've

14

watered the plants. Sometimes, what looks like a memory problem is really a hearing and attention-deficit problem. That works for me. I'd rather have a hearing problem than a memory problem, thank you very much.

I asked Dr. D. if I could take anything—some drug-based cognitive enhancement that could improve my memory and attention. If there were, I might be interested. But he said a healthy lifestyle was the drug he would recommend for both brain and body.

I don't belong to a gym or health club, but I do walk two miles several times a week and live a somewhat out-of-the-box active lifestyle for a woman of my age. For example, two winters ago our two-and-a-half-story barn collapsed in a heavy snowstorm. During the course of the past year I, along with my adult son and daughter-in-law, have taken the barn completely down, using one maul, an electric chain saw, and an axe. I loved the challenge, the reward of seeing the barn disappear over time, and the physicality of the work. I'm fairly well toned for someone who's sixty-five and doesn't go to a gym.

Like our bodies, our brains need stimulation to remain fit. For lovers of travel this is excellent news. Our brains like us to go to museums, listen to music, and meet new people. Taking up a new language or traveling in a foreign country functions as an intellectual push-up.

I don't have any imminent plans to go around the world or take a class in Mandarin or applied mathematics. But I have always had what felt like an irrational prejudice that keeping up with technology in the twenty-first century is essential if I want to stay alert and connected. I was an early PalmPilot and Kindle adopter. Each of these came with a learning curve. Nowadays I still always trade up for the latest smartphone. Every group has an individual in it that will pull their phone out at the mere hint of a question. I am that person. (I read online that this puts me at risk for developing a new syndrome called the Google effect: the tendency to forget information that can be easily found online. I will risk this syndrome.)

My urge to stay technologically current runs deeper than wanting the latest toy (although wanting toys is somewhat true). For me, the push not to be technologically left behind has something to do with fearing the isolation that comes from an aging brain.

Technology is my growth area. It is my foreign language. I refuse to be left behind by technological change without a fight. As I have aged I have seen person after person drop out of the technological learning curve. Tim, in his late eighties, refused to get an answering machine. That's where he drew the line. Jill won't switch to a cellular phone. Libby stopped at the smartphone.

So when the cover of today's *Wired* magazine tells me that some twenty-one-year-old kid with the fabulous name of Palmer Luckey has invented a virtual reality headset called the Oculus Rift, I'm interested. Virtual reality is expected to change *everything* from education to art to travel to entertainment and even to medicine in the next few years. That's a lot of learning curve—very good for the brain.

Enzo, my twenty-two-month-old grandson, has no television in his home but knows his way around an iPad like an old pro. Not bad for a young man of his age (a true compliment in this case). We have always had a special bond that is evident not just to me but to everyone who sees us together. When he was a bit younger, and a month or two would pass before I'd see him again, I always worried that he wouldn't remember who I was. I needn't have. He's got a good little memory going for him. I think it's fair to say that he's sharp as a tack.

I would like to hitchhike quietly along with Enzo and his generation in the decades to come, not only because I can't get enough of my grandson but also because I want to position myself in a place where I can see reality continue to morph, and I'm sure he will make a great tour guide. When he comes to visit he'll know where to find me. I'll be the one out back in the garden, wearing the latest version of the virtual reality headset.

A Witness to Life, Death, and Then

CARL SCOVEL

> Lord, let me know my end,
> and what is the measure of my days;
> let me know how fleeting my life is.
>
> PSALM 39:4

What a strange, sad, hard, but, above all, good time is this, the autumn of our lives, this elderhood, old age, retirement, Erikson's eighth stage and Shakespeare's sixth age of life, this penultimate chapter, this final chance to learn!

For those of us blessed with health and some energy, it's an active time. It's a time for still sweeping the floors, shoveling the steps, paying bills, a time for phone calls, emails, reading, walks, naps, funerals. In my case, there is still time for counseling, teaching, tai chi, eulogies, watching grandsons play hockey and futsal, and walking others home from school. Like other retirees, I say, "I don't know why I'm so busy."

Despite the busyness, however, another life abides, a life within, a life from which I look out, take note, reflect, remember, muse, inquire, and pray. Freed from earning my living, unlike some my age, I have time to see and consider as I never had before.

Without this exploration I would experience boredom or despair. These interchanges between my inner and outer worlds are energizing, mind-, soul-, heart-, and body-widening. I can't imagine living any other way—at this time.

Strangely, perhaps, I am free to feel what seem like negative emotions.

I am free to feel regret. I look back on my mistakes, on my sins, on my blindness to family and friends and to my real self. I don't excuse myself or beat myself up. These events are still part of my life now. I hope that I never forget them and will always be learning from them.

I am also free to feel sadness, for this is a time of loss. We lose energy, ambition, illusions, hair, teeth, vision, hopes, as well as friends, kin, and colleagues. I am sad at what I never accomplished in my ministry and sad over the pain in so many people's lives, especially in those I know.

But I know it's right to be sad at such loss and pain. I'd rather be sad than depressed, for sadness frees me from depression, which is repressed grief and energy turned inward.

At this time I also feel apprehension—about the constant turning of people to fear, anger, blame, and violence. I feel apprehension about my children's and grandchildren's futures, about the possible death of loved ones—"the sudden silence in the next room," as someone put it. And, of course, I feel apprehension about my own dying and diminishment and how I'll deal with Shakespeare's seventh stage.

All these feelings and what prompts them are real. They're part of being alive in elderhood, but one more feeling outweighs all the ones I've just described—gratitude. Time and again I'm struck with how good life has been to me or, to put it from my heart, how generous God has been.

Just to be alive, to have been born eighty-one years ago, "lifted from the no of all nothing," as E. E. Cummings puts it, and not just once but again and again in a series of small resurrections, raised from depression, stupidity, self-absorption, and the service of false gods, reborn every morning and given a whole new day. These are blessings beyond any payback.

Blessings, yes!—for all the years my wife and I have lived together and all we've learned together; blessings, for our wonderful offspring and their spouses and their offspring; for brothers and sisters, their families, and dear, dear friends. Cares and concerns come with all these relationships, but who would we be without them?

Retired from the parish, I found a congregation whose humanity and piety, intelligence and solidarity, drew me to them, as well as their liturgy ("industrial-strength Christianity," said one member) and their wise, educated, and humane priest. In their company I'm glad to be a layman.

I'm grateful for my colleagues of the last fifty years, whom I see in groups or individually. They are still teaching me from their experience and reflections.

But all this is going to end someday. The psalmist says, "Let me know my end." I don't know when or how or where, but it will happen. That someday could be today, tomorrow, next week, next month, who knows? But someday I will be knowing what I am writing about now in a far more real way.

I will be living my departure from this world—this world that I so dearly love: the hills and woods I've walked, the songs I've sung and heard, the beer

I've drunk and the bread I've baked and eaten, the conversations with my friends and colleagues, the embraces of my wife and all we've done, discussed, and decided together, our dear offspring and their families, the liturgies at church. All these and so much more. When I think of my end, I feel great sadness at the prospect of losing life on this wonderful and sometimes terrible world.

I don't anticipate a death with dignity. I've seen too much of death in hospitals and streets and homes. As an orderly, I prepared the bodies of the dead for the undertaker. As a minister, I blessed the bodies of many parishioners before the undertaker arrived. As a son, I prayed over my father's body in the morgue, having watched him through six months of dying. Dignity? Perhaps for a lucky few, but not most of us, I think.

But dying is not the point for me at this moment. My question is, And then? As Robert G. Ingersoll writes, every coffin asks us, "Whither?" How do we answer that question? Do we say heaven or nowhere or who knows? Whatever we say, we all face that question.

I stand witness and I confess that I was born in goodness, that I have been guided all my life by goodness, though I often did not heed that guidance. I witness that I was and am nourished and sustained by goodness, corrected by goodness, and called by goodness to trust a future that rationally and experientially I cannot know. Indeed, I believe it is good that I do not know what lies ahead and therefore have to trust the goodness I've known in this world, and by grace was part of—an unending goodness of which we are all part.

The psalmist says "Lord, let me know my end." That end is not just the cessation of my life but the purpose of my life as well, the purpose God intended in my creation. That intent can never be fulfilled in a single lifetime but only in what follows a lifetime, both here on earth and in my return to that goodness by which we were born.

Does this goodness spare me pain, sadness, regret, apprehension, and an undignified dying? Of course not. But it promises that as my life has meaning, so does my death. My death is part of my completion, though I cannot see or understand how at this time.

All this lies ahead and cannot be my main concern for now. While I am here, there are bills to be paid, floors to be swept, bread to be baked, boys to be walked home from school, books to be read and prayers to be said, this essay to be finished, and in W. H. Auden's words "the Time Being to be redeemed from insignificance." For this and so much more, what can I say but thanks be to God.

Postscript: Writing a P.S. to an essay like this is unusual, but the above leads me to think about my funeral. It will not be titled "A Celebration of the Life of Carl Scovel." Although I won't be there, I hope the memorial words will be modest and accurate.

There will be a casket present so that the congregation knows experientially that someone actually died. The congregation will sing the great hymns of mourning, prayer, and praise. They will hear great texts that deal with the mystery and solemnity of our departure from this world. The funeral service will include a confession so that the people have a chance to forgive me for the harm I did to them or to confess the harm they think they did to me. There will be prayers, of course, and the commendation of my soul to whatever disposition God has chosen for it.

By the end of the service I hope they will know that they have together faced death's great question mark and Christ's promise of the life that lies beyond. More than this I could not ask for.

Beginner's Mind

MAUREEN KILLORAN

I feel like I'm too old to be a beginner. Common sense says we are all beginners, but that's not how it seems in the everyday world. Groceries to buy? I know how to do that. Emails to send? Orders of service to draft? Check, check. I've been there and done that—in some cases, hundreds or even thousands of times. In my everyday world, I am busy, at times overworked, but I am not a beginner. Or at least it rarely feels that way.

And now, on the threshold of my eighth decade, I have a choice. Will I continue as long as possible doing what I have always done in my familiar ways? Or will I take a leap—yes, a leap of faith—and throw myself into the unknown? Believing these questions to be of profound importance, gerontologist Ken Dychtwald writes, "How we decide to behave as elders will, in all likelihood,

27

become the most important challenge we will face in our lives."

For me, these challenges—and the choices that follow—are deeply spiritual. I hear echoes of my midlife question, What do I want to be when I grow up? Now, however, something deeper is at work. I don't have the unlimited amounts of time that seemed ahead at fifty, nor are my choices as vast as they appeared when I was thirty. Time is shorter, options increasingly limited, and I suspect that *what* is not the right question anyway.

Retirement pundits stress the importance of knowing what you want to do, where you want to do it, and how you're going to pay for it—decisions that could affect as much as forty years of your life. Of course, much of this kind of advice is based on the privileged assumption that you have saved money or will receive a pension, and that you have the financial and physical flexibility to make long-term decisions and follow through on them. I have these things in a limited way, and I am both amazed and grateful for that. Still, when I consider the conventional wisdom, I see primarily the *what* question: What do I want to do when I retire?

But I feel called to focus less on the pragmatics of *what* and more on the intangible question of *who*: Who do I hope to be (and become)? And the related questions: What song does my spirit want to sing? How can I best open my heart to the untested energy of the new?

These are not easy questions for someone who has taken pride in her moderate professional success, who some say has *Control* as her middle name. As I write this, I hear an inner voice protest: "Look what I've done, the odds I've overcome! You can't mean I should leave all that behind, turn completely away?" Indeed, others who hear similar inner voices, will not want to reevaluate their identities at this point in their lives. But I am coming to believe it may be a spiritual imperative for me.

I recall the Zen student who had mastered every program that had come her way. Convinced she was ready to move on, she accepted her teacher's invitation to share some tea. "Hold out your cup," the teacher said. He poured and poured until the student's cup was full, until tea ran down the side and onto the floor. "Stop!" cried the student. "My cup overflows." "So it is with your life," said the teacher. "When your cup is already filled, you cannot learn something new."

As the twentieth-century Zen master Shunryu Suzuki said, "In the beginner's mind there are many possibilities, but in the expert's there are few."

And yet, it still feels like I'm too old to be a beginner. I could keep on doing more of the same things I've been doing, at least for the foreseeable future, and all the while I'll still be me. This is good, but it is not sufficient. I dream of something new, an exploration, an expansion of spirit.

It's time to more consistently raise my eyes from the horizon—each time I do, I remember the banner hanging above my desk. I've seen that banner every day since someone left it in my office, yet today its message touches more deeply:

> In the end, what matters most is
>> How well did you live
>> How well did you love
>> How well did you learn to let go.

A message literally written on my wall: How well did I learn to let go? That's a beginner kind of question, because letting go of one thing requires opening to the new. It's scary, makes me feel humble. Then I recall that *humility* and *human* are etymological cousins. Perhaps to be successfully human in my next life chapter, I must embrace humility, must accept and even rejoice in who I am: a woman with a young heart. A woman who is nonetheless growing old.

I would be disingenuous to pretend that aging is not ultimately about endings. I've companioned too many people though their final days not to know, in my spirit and in my bones, that my body will continue the deterioration of which I am already well aware. Pain that is manageable now may not always stay that way. My grandmother died with Alzheimer's disease, so there's more than a chance that I will too. Sooner or later it will be my turn, or—unbearable to consider—the turn of my beloved spouse, to die. Sooner or later, but not yet.

Right now, there's work to be done. To be a genuine beginner, I need to shed my decades-long habits of over functioning and being controlling. Belatedly I take to heart the note given me by a congregant in the first church I served: "Remember, you are not responsible for absolutely everything. That's my job. Love, from God."

Think about it. If I'm really not responsible for everything, then I have to trust, at least in terms of what the Universe is sending my way. And so I say a prayer, maybe best addressed as To Whom It May Concern:

In humility, I acknowledge that I don't know where the road is going to lead.

By intention, I choose to trust that life's gifts will surprise me.

By faith, I choose to believe that, in the face of life's challenges, I will find the strength I need.

Should I say "Amen"? I don't think so. This is my *life*, not a prayer that is ending, at least not yet. Now, as a beginner on the threshold of my end zone, I simply pray that I may embrace my next unknown with humility and trust. If my choices bring joy to my heart and, in a small way, contribute to the balance of justice and love in the world, then I will have succeeded.

Rise in Body or in Spirit

WILLIAM SINKFORD

Becoming an elder was never my goal. Over the years I have looked at older men, older than I am, and thought, "Someday that might be me." I don't remember those moments as being either frightening or depressing. I never really inhabited that future. I don't remember projecting myself into a time when aging would be an important part of my living. Old age was an inevitable destination, if I lived to deal with it, but it was never a goal. Truth be told, I don't think I ever took aging seriously or personally. Until recent years.

I remember looking at those older men, noticing their beginning or advancing fragility, the tentativeness in their step, their thinning legs, their etched faces, the age spots. I noticed the signs of their physical aging and, until recently, I conveniently stored those images away. I wasn't dealing with those losses, those reductions in strength and ability. The myth of invincibility in young men (and young people generally) that so many comment upon remained with me until recent years.

Now I am sixty-eight—*young*, in terms of popular culture so much influenced by my baby-boom generation and industries that cater to the large number of those my age. "Seventy is the new fifty," they say. Yes . . . and no. There most certainly is life, love, and productivity at seventy and well beyond. But we are dealing with changes too.

Changes to that eighteen-year-old body I remember: that trim, graceful body I had when I fantasized of a career as a professional tennis star. Changes to that thirty-five-year-old body I remember: that well-muscled, construction-worker body I had when I ran a small business renovating homes and churches. Those body images are not just memory. They still live in me. The body I see in the mirror today feels less certainly me than either of those earlier bodies.

For many years, I have understood myself to be middle-aged. But I just don't know many 140-year-olds. So much of popular culture seems to focus on denial of aging rather than embracing its reality. Even to use the phrase *embracing the reality of aging* highlights the dilemma. Aging is about decreased ability, increased limitation, reduced independence, increased reliance on others. Aging is about the acceptance of approaching death. Why would anyone embrace aging? Isn't the only sane approach to resist it?

I have lived a lucky life so far, in many ways. One way I have been most fortunate, blessed really, is that I have always been able to rely on my body. My tall, strong, male body was a given. To understand how privileged that body has made me has been the work of a lifetime. I had a few injuries and routine sicknesses over the years, but I always recovered quickly and completely. Nothing happened to me that Western medicine could not fix. The myth of invincibility remained intact.

Then, at age fifty-six, during a routine physical, my doctor felt what *might be* some abnormalities on my prostate. "Probably nothing to worry about, but it would be a good idea to have that checked out." In the biopsy they discovered cancer.

When I got the call, I was in San Francisco, two hours before a major presentation where I had to show up with my A game. I was in a state of shock. Thankfully, I had the good sense not to keep the news to myself. I asked a colleague for five minutes of pastoral care. His calm and caring presence helped.

Most helpful, however, was his sharing what he knew about the disease, which made it clear that I needed to learn about this cancer. I had a task to take on, and I knew how to deal with tasks. Putting learning about prostate cancer on my to-do list allowed me to get through the presentation. I used my skills at compartmentalization at a level that surprised even me.

Luckily, the cancer had not developed too far. I received consultations about treatment options, second and third opinions, and successful treatment.

It was a wake-up call. *Cancer* is one of those big, frightening words. I learned how little I knew about its many forms, how little attention I had paid. Most men, at least in the West, will develop prostate cancer if they live long enough. It apparently comes with the testosterone. If diagnosed early, the success rates for treatment are very high. If it is diagnosed early. I will be forever grateful to my internist for catching the early signs of the cancer in that routine screening.

I initially kept the diagnosis quite private—not out of shame, or at least not exactly out of shame. I was president of the Unitarian Universalist Association at the time. I thought my ministry in that capacity would somehow be compromised if word got out that I had cancer. However, what I feared most was the sympathy. Sympathy directed my way makes me squirm. It challenges my self-image as a person who is in control and able to manage just fine, thank you very much.

After successful treatment, however, I allowed my name, face, and story to be used in a campaign by Beth Israel Deaconess Medical Center in Boston, where my surgery was done, to increase awareness of this disease. It felt like the least I could do.

I've been cancer-free for a dozen years now. It is unlikely that prostate cancer will kill me. But the disease did cause me to confront death in a more direct and personal way, especially before I knew much about the disease. The not knowing was the killer.

Like the outcome of the injuries and illness of my younger years, the treatment was successful, the recovery complete. I experienced some change in my sexual function but no elimination of desire. I had incontinence that was treated medically. The focus of my fear, however, was not the threat to my life itself but the threat to my life as a sexual being.

The changes as a result of the treatment were modest. And I had never had symptoms that I attributed, even with hindsight, to the cancer. I was able to return, chastened perhaps, to that myth of invincibility.

A few years later, however, I took a fall exiting a small commuter plane in South Carolina. The bruising was extensive, but I soldiered on. In the next weeks and months, my walking became more and more compromised, and the pain got worse, not better.

I underwent surgery to alleviate the pain. But my walking and my balance never returned. The final diagnosis was neuropathy. Though that term has a fancy medical definition, what it means to me is that the nerves to my feet and lower legs don't work right.

Exercise and physical therapy, acupuncture, and extra vitamins help. I now wear braces on both legs to correct the drop in my feet. I walk slowly and awkwardly, and when I have to stand in one place, I need to place my hand on a friendly shoulder or wall. It makes receptions and receiving lines . . . well, let's just say I don't enjoy them nearly as much as I once did.

The Western medical community tells me, and I have come to accept, that there is no cure. I won't get better. Over time, there will be some degradation in my abilities. I hate that thought and fear the time when I may not be able to walk or stand on my own.

At General Assembly, the large annual gathering of Unitarian Universalists, I began using a scooter to get around. I simply couldn't walk fast enough to get from location to location within the time frames of the conference. The scooter was easy enough to justify while I was still working through diagnosis and treatment options, easy to justify as I was recovering from the surgery. Now, it is just what I need to do.

Accepting my new physical reality has been a test, and it is still a work in progress. I don't use a scooter at home or at work. I don't use a cane or anything. Part of the reason is my fear that using an assist of any kind would encourage my congregation to begin *taking care* of me, which would compromise my ability to care for and minister to them. That is a real concern. But pride is also involved. And pride can be dangerous.

I also know, or at least believe, that once I begin using more assistive devices, I'll never return to life without them. So I refuse to use them.

The rational part of me, which continues to function well (at least as far as I can tell), knows that my congregation sees me walk awkwardly. I have never fallen in public, but they know.

Worse, using a visible assist would make me feel that the end is near, or at least nearing, even if that wasn't the case. The invincible younger man inside me, who never had to think about physical limitations, who could rely on his body to do what he asked it to do, who never had to think about limitations or compromises, resents these limitations and, when I allow him to, rails against them.

I live with a sense of betrayal. The body I relied on for so many years is letting me down. I am still mad about it. Furious, actually. How is it possible to be so angry at my own body, at myself?

My mind seems uncompromised by aging, at least so far. But there are qualifications even to that statement. My memory is not as sharp as it once was. I need to make more notes, lest I forget things. That doesn't feel like much of a compromise.

Yet my spirit seems to deepen by the day.

The spirit is willing, but the body? A quip from the used car business comes to mind: "It's not the mileage but the wear and tear on the chassis that matters."

I am blessed to be doing a ministry I love. I now serve as the minister at First Unitarian, Portland,

Oregon, and four years in, parish ministry is proving to be just as satisfying as I imagined it would. I loved my time at the UUA. I gave everything I had to that work. But now I am finally living out the call to ministry I heard and answered twenty-five years ago.

What takes a toll is the having to pay attention, almost all the time: needing to plan where I can stand, calculating how far I can walk. How close can I park to that meeting? How many steps will I have to climb? How long will I have to stand?

My colleagues at the church increasingly understand that I have limitations. They are both gracious and generous in making accommodations without making a big production of it. No one asks me to march in protests. I just show up at the speakers' platform at the end of the march. We've modified our child dedication ritual so that I don't hold the children. I need to place a hand on someone's shoulder to stand and sing the hymns.

At a recent installation where I preached, I decided to take the invitation to "rise in body or spirit" seriously and remained seated. It felt like a watershed moment. Could I give myself permission to acknowledge my limitations so publicly? I found out, of course, that the world continued spinning on its axis while I remained seated to sing. It was not a big deal to anyone other than me.

It felt like another step in acceptance of who I am now. A healthy decision, no doubt. The problem is that more such decisions will surely be required, and each one presents the same spiritual test. Each one presents yet another opportunity to accept a new, more limited body. Each one calls up again the sense of betrayal, the anger, and the disappointment.

What is hardest to accept is not any one sign of the reality of my physical limitations, but the knowledge that dealing with them will be part of my life for the rest of my life.

One positive result of having those questions always on my mind is that I have found a new and much more personal sensitivity to issues of disability in general. I always thought I was mindful of those issues and supported folks who deal with physical and mental limitations, but those issues have moved way up my list of priorities. And I realize that my story is about the loss of being fully functional, not the story of living with a disability for a lifetime or a long time.

I am a minister, so I sometimes try theological reflection to help me deal with my new reality. I believe not that we have bodies but that we are bodies. I don't believe there is some soul separate from the physical embodiment of Bill Sinkford. No essence of Bill separate from the presence of Bill. Yet, it is tempting to think of my body only as a container for the real me, that although my body will inevitably deteriorate and finally die, my essence will live on.

Death is not far underneath all my wrestling with these changes in my body. Not fear of death, because, to date, I haven't experienced fear about my life ending. Perhaps that will come at some point. The challenge is living with the reality that death is the final destination, the end point, at least as we can know for certain. It is knowing not only that death is inevitable but also that it is right and even good.

Part of ministry—some would say the most important and meaningful part—is being with congregants as they are dying, and being with family members and friends as they deal with the loss, the grief, even the anger they experience as their loved ones die. As I age, I find I am bringing something different to those moments. Whatever acceptance I am finding of my own mortality is a gift I can offer, rarely in words, but in easiness, perhaps even gracefulness—*grace-filledness*—that I hope communicates and somehow consoles.

Becoming an elder was never something I aspired to become or shaped my life around. I cannot remember it changing a single important decision I've made.

However, undeniably, an elder is what I am becoming. I know this in part because of the care others take to make sure I am comfortable. My children, my wife, my colleagues, the person who stands to offer me a seat, the bellperson at the hotel who asks, "Can I help you with that, young man?" I increasingly welcome that care and those offers.

People also seem to be coming to me for wisdom, asking me to share what I have learned from the long experience of living. How to respond? In my younger years, when I knew so much more, the temptation was to tell people what to do. I am thankful that I have, for the most part, grown out of such arrogance. And my ministerial calling helps me remember that the greatest gift I can offer is to hear people into their own speech.

Still, I've learned some things, things that my experience leads me to believe I know. Those life lessons are best communicated by sharing my stories. I know that. But there is a balance required; so in addition to the stories I find that I offer advice and counsel too. I am still actively and happily working. I make decisions every day. I am not yet at the stage where telling my story is all I have to offer or all I am required to do.

Being present to myself as I age is my primary discipline. Although I study and learn from the stories and examples of so many men and women who have moved through this phase of life, this aging process feels huge. It feels important to do it well. And it feels like it will require all the honesty and as much courage as I can muster to navigate it well.

A Woman of Worth

LYNN THOMAS STRAUSS

My Indiana cousin recently sent me a black and white photo taken in 1944, the year I was born. My great-grandparents were making a rare visit to Chicago from the farm where my maternal grandfather was born and raised. There I was, in the photo, barely five months old, squirming unhappily on my great-grandfather's lap. My brother, just eleven months older, was scowling as our great-grandmother held him firmly in place on her lap.

Also in the photo were my grandparents, my aunt and uncle, two young cousins, and there in the back row, clearly wishing they were someplace else, stood my parents. My father, muscular and tan, looking tough with his shirt collar turned up and his hair slicked back, and my mother, in a brightly patterned, close-fitting dress, leaning into Dad with a hand on her hip; they looked like movie stars, both of them beautiful, vibrant, working-class teenagers.

My parents' marriage was a great romance, and mother grew more beautiful as the years passed. I've never looked anything like my mother. She was slim and tall with naturally wavy, beautiful red hair. Her skin was as white and delicate as a flower. I, on the other hand, was sturdy, with dark skin and straight dark hair that my mother was forever trying to curl. I'll never forget the smell of those home perms and the hours I spent on the kitchen chair, newspaper covering the floor, my eyes burning. She wanted me to look like Shirley Temple.

Mother remained the beauty of the family. As I moved through girlhood into adolescence, I read many coming-of-age stories. I escaped into reading, hungry to know how it would feel to be pretty, whether it was possible to be both pretty and capable, whether I could be pretty, capable, and smart. I searched for a reflection of myself, but none seemed to fit.

American culture doesn't offer a vision of what it might mean to be a woman of worth. And so the political, religious, and economic debates continue to swirl in the daily media around women's roles, women's rights, women's sexuality, women's bodies, and women's place. And the patriarchal foundation of our country and culture continue to dominate attitudes and expectations and behaviors of boys and girls, women and men.

When I was young, I wanted to be good. I tried to be a good daughter, a good sister, a good student, a good person. If I couldn't be pretty, I thought, at least I could be good. But it wasn't always easy.

I remember the torturous decisions of how much makeup to wear, what skirt length was stylish but not too sexy, how to wear my hair. Trying to figure it all out, trying to find myself, I hung out with different crowds, testing the limit of my goodness, with decidedly risky behavior. After several emotionally abusive relationships in my early twenties, after the sorrow and trauma of a late-term, illegal abortion, I survived to meet and marry a good man.

At twenty-nine I became a parent. I was immediately conscious of the life and death responsibility of being a mother. I carried this heavy awareness through the raising of four children. Accepting the life-giving responsibility of motherhood brought me great personal satisfaction and a sense of well-being and value. I had found my way to worth. Whatever the societal prejudices regarding motherhood, it was for me, as for many women, an experience of positive self-actualization.

During the times of pregnancies and nursing I felt most strong, most healthy, most beautiful, and most alive. Parenting came easily to me and was a source of power and purpose. I also knew that the time of parenting would come to an end and I wanted a career that would offer a similar experience of power and purpose. I intended to continue my life as a woman of worth.

When my fourth child was two years old, I began a divinity degree program. I was ordained into the Unitarian Universalist ministry at forty-seven. Entering ministry in midlife as the first woman minister to serve my congregation in Knoxville, Tennessee, had various implications related to age and gender. I worried about whether the pitch of my voice would be too high or sound grating. I wished I could wear a suit and tie like my male colleagues and not have to show my legs or wear shoes with high heels. On Sunday mornings congregants often commented on what I was wearing. I still had to make those decisions about how much makeup, what length skirt, and how to wear my hair. I also found it wise, over the next few years, to dye my graying hair to avoid being seen as too old—this, while male colleagues were seen as wise and distinguished for having white hair. And as women of any age are often objectified and sexualized in our culture, I needed to be most careful with language, necklines, and humor and to take care when offering pastoral care to men.

Fortunately, for most of my twenty-four years in ministry, I have been perceived as younger than my years. My energy and health are good, but now that my husband is retired and I approach the age of seventy, perhaps I need to come clean about my age and throw myself a boisterous birthday party. I wonder if some in my congregation are thinking it is time for a younger minister. Being a professional and a mother and grandmother is a kind of sleight of hand at times; one too many photos of grandchildren or cute stories shared in a sermon might lead to my professional demise. So I'm careful to talk loudly about my tennis game and the theology books I'm reading.

I love being a mother and a grandmother, but is it possible in our culture to be a professional and a bit overweight and a proud-as-punch grandmother and still be granted dignity and value?

And if motherhood is the pivotal experience of many women's worth, who do we become when our primary maternal tasks are completed? Does "empty nest" imply an empty brain, an empty future? Now that women are living far beyond their mothering years and then also celebrating long careers, what comes next? Does an old woman still have worth? When she is seventy-five, eighty-five, or ninety-five?

As I've pondered these questions, I have returned again and again to the Hebrew Bible and the book of Ruth. The story of Ruth and Naomi is a woman's tale told in a man's world. It is a story of survival, of life overcoming death, of choice. It is a story of two women of different ages—both women of worth.

Naomi and Ruth were foreigners in a patriarchal land. As widowed women, they depended on men for their survival. Naomi, the older woman, was Ruth's mother-in-law. She advised Ruth to return to her homeland. Ruth refused to leave Naomi, trusting that together they would find shelter in the land of Judah.

Ruth, a foreigner, a stranger in the land of Judah, acted with courage and agency when she linked her future, her very life, with Naomi. "Where you go I will go; . . . your people shall be my people and your God my God. Where you die, I will die— there will I be buried."

Rather than pledge her life to a father, a brother, or a husband, Ruth binds herself to a mother figure. This is a radical choice representing radical hope. Ruth sees Naomi as a woman of worth, an elder who will protect her and who she also will help. She makes a covenantal statement that proves true. Together they survive and thrive. Radical choices continue throughout the story, culminating in the marriage of Ruth to Boaz and the conception of a son, who becomes the progenitor of the future King David.

The significance of Ruth's role in this lineage is underscored by the story's ending, in which, after Ruth gives birth, Naomi lifts the child up and the women of the village offer a blessing by choosing his name. This is a blessing of older women honoring the worth of the younger woman. A mother honoring a daughter.

As I age I feel more sure of my mother's love. Several years ago she gave me a ring, a single red glass stone set high in a plain gold band. I remember seeing this shiny ring on my mother's hand every day of my childhood. The story of the ring is that my father found the stone among his mother's things after she died and had it made into a ring for my mother. They thought it was a gemstone. But my mother learned it was mere glass, and guessed that my grandpa had won it in a card game. The worth of the ring is not found in its resale value but as a symbol of the covenant of family love.

The ring I now wear carries the story of my grandfather's win at cards, my grandmother's too-early death from cancer, my parents' great romance, and, at long last, my mother's blessing upon me. Every day I look at my mother's ring on my no-longer-young hand and smile. For the first time in my life, I feel her blessing. In the ring I see a reflection of her looking back at me as if she's seeing me for the first time. In quiet moments, I entertain the possibility that she always thought I was beautiful. I am grateful that I have lived long enough to know that she is a woman of worth. And that she knows I am as well.

Memento Mori

BURTON D. CARLEY

The room is darkened and quiet except for the occasional beep from the ultrasound machine. If it were not for the term *exploration*, I could have drifted off to sleep. I have always thought of myself as an explorer, leaving the familiar for the unknown. In the rearview mirror of my life I can see the litter of inheritance discarded for the evolution of the spirit. Once I told the congregation I have served for thirty-one years that my dream settlement would be chaplain aboard the starship *Enterprise*. It is why I joined the Unitarian Universalist faith community—for us, exploration is the norm.

The young technician disturbs my contemplation. "Breathe in and hold it," she says. Her voice is calm, almost soothing. "Breathe out" is a welcomed permission. I think it strange to feel gratitude, as if

I've passed some test. All the while, another part of me is aware of a rising anxiety.

I use reason as a levee against that tide, to give me security. An image from my office comes to mind. It is a plaque given as a gift by a colleague. It reads, "All shall be well." Odd, I think, because I had often argued with Julian of Norwich's affirmation, having learned in my profession that it is wise to imagine how things might go wrong. As Ralph Waldo Emerson says, "There is a crack in everything God has made." I knew it to be true in institutional life and in the lives of my parishioners. The problem is that everything included me.

I feel the paddles sliding across my abdomen, stopping here and there and being pressed down. The diagnostic procedure seems to be taking a long time. The tide rises higher against the levee. The technician asks, "Now, why did the doctor send you for this examination?" I wonder if something surprising is displayed on the screen. The problem with this kind of exploration is that you are looking for something you really don't want to find, something that changes everything, something that finally tells you what you have always known but do not want to experience—your mortality. A phrase comes to mind: *memento mori*, the reminder that we all must die.

This might seem curious for a parish minister, who through a long career has conducted so many funerals and graveside services, prayed by hospital beds, and counseled the terminally ill. Disease, accidents, and the slow unwinding of body or mind are all too common. I do not need a skull in my study to remind me of human fragility and transience. The title of a reading in our hymnal swam into consciousness: *We were never meant to survive*. Was this reason or anxiety speaking?

The technician waits for my answer. "Fatty liver, gallstones. I don't know. Exploratory exam recommended with the physical." Exploration not of an idea or a place or a culture but of my body. Definitely less exciting. We don't always get to explore what we want. Sometimes things come to us unbidden though natural. We are given by time new territory to explore. My territory was aging and approaching retirement. At the moment I felt out to sea with the safety of the shore receding a little too fast in the distance.

The technician offers no response. She continues the procedure as each minute passes more slowly than the next. Finally she stops. I don't want to feel relief, the need for it, but I do. Unfortunately, it was premature. The technician asks me to remain on the table. She needs to leave the room to speak to a colleague and will return shortly. Then she is gone.

Alone in the subdued examination room the tension between anxiety and reason reaches a new level. No longer do I need to feign composure, at least to myself. Either the technician discovered something and needs advice on how to proceed or I am about to make medical history, and future students will look at bizarre ultrasound images of my organs in their textbooks. Reason, donning a persona I know well as the wise pastor, counsels me not to project.

The door opens and the youthful technician comes back, and she is not alone. A senior colleague is with her. In a confident voice clothed in the comfortable tenor of authority, the mature technician informs me that she is going to repeat the ultrasound.

The new technician is smart about her business. No lingering. She offers instruction to her colleague in a low voice. Then it occurs to me that the first technician was new at her work. Maybe that is why, good reason rejoins, the procedure is taking so long. Yes, maybe, all shall be well.

Then I hear a word I don't like. The supervisor stops the motion of the paddles and presses

down. "See that?" she asks. "It is probably a polyp."
I silently roll the word *polyp* off my tongue as if it is
a foreign word I must master. I search for the significance of the term without success.

My anxiety is fully empowered now and provides an analogy. The polyp is like an iceberg and
I am on the *Titanic*. Reason pleads to stop this non-
sense, but anxiety is already sounding the alarm
bell. Abandon ship! I know how this ends. Few
escape. A small blue plastic ice tray appears in my
mind. Another gift, and it resides at this moment
in the freezer at home. The ice from the tray does
not come out in a cube but in the shapes of an iceberg and the *Titanic*. There, floating in my gin, is
memento mori.

Reason staggers. It clings to the word *probably*
and puts it on like a life jacket. *Probably* is not a
definite term; there is room for doubt. Then comes
an angelic pronouncement. The exam is over.

I'm allowed to sit up, and I ask for a towel to
clean off the remaining lotion. The attending technician asks me to wait while she shows the results
to a physician. Now I interpret every move, every
voice inflection for clues to my fate. Why must a
hospital doctor read my results instead of sending
the report to my primary-care physician? Is some-

thing urgent? I would rather hear bad news from someone I know.

The technician returns and tells me I can go. The results of the ultrasound will be sent to my doctor who will explain them. The mystery of the hour is not solved. Yet even as I try not to dwell on what needs to be explained, I experience a wave of release. Limbo seems a pleasant vacation. I would never say that ignorance is bliss, but as a respite it does nicely.

I walk out of the hospital doing the jig of an escaped convict. No doubt I will be caught and sent back. The feeling of freedom, however, is intoxicating.

As I get into my car I notice how famished I am. I could not eat or drink the evening before the ultrasound. It is now late morning and I decide to treat myself to breakfast on the way to the office. I order a short stack, two eggs over easy, and bacon.

Bacon is unusual for me. Restricting that delight from my diet was a small nod toward health. The waitress asks, "Two slices or three?" Something in how I say *three* amuses her. She smiles. Breakfast never tasted so good, and I wonder if the bread dipped in the dish at the last supper tasted as delicious. *Memento mori*.

I put the whole episode behind me and do what I normally do when troubled. I concentrate on work and domestic tasks. All of a sudden I possess energy to do things that procrastination had prevented me from. My defense mechanism does have benefits.

One, two, three days pass and no call from my doctor. Those who love me ask, "Did he phone yet?" They encourage me to call. I resist, as reason reassures me that no news is good news. Anxiety resorts to name calling. Reason is a wimp and I'm in denial. Later I learn that my doctor was out of the country on vacation. On a Monday, five days after the ultrasound, I get the call.

Reason cautions me not to jump to conclusions. Anxiety counsels me to be prepared for the worst. Tired of that bickering dialogue, I feel a peace settle over me. I will now know; and if all cannot be well, it will be okay, for I am in this moment what I have always been: a student. I would learn once again what life had to teach me, even if I was not eager for the lesson.

The diagnosis is carefully explained so not to exaggerate or cause undue alarm. It is not life threatening and a minimalist plan of treatment is suggested. The polyp is of no concern.

The next week a different experience of *memento mori* takes place. I am having lunch with a parishioner, and on the way out of the restaurant a colleague from the First Presbyterian Church stops me to say hello. He says, "I hear you are retiring." Anxiety hears instead, "See, you are a lame-duck minister." Reason replies, "Don't listen. You are at the top of your game."

I expect that when I retire I will experience a sweetness about the decades of work so challenging and rewarding. I will breathe a sigh, having managed that high-wire act without falling. I will also be happy not to attend another meeting or feel the pressure of another canvass. However, I also anticipate experiencing feelings similar to the ultrasound exam: facing the unknown, the movement from what is to what if to what now.

I pray that as I age I can learn to refuse the internal drama created by medical exams and the outward prospect of needing the pulse and attention of a public career. I pray that what I have preached is true, that we are saved through our humanity and not in spite of it.

Memento mori. Everything ends. Our lives, our positions, everything we cherish. Even the good earth will end some day. We shall lose everything, and I'm convinced that we can take nothing with us at the end. This is the human condition, which reality keeps reminding me I am part of.

Yet, for all the trouble of being born and having to die, there is a saving grace: the possibility of the evolution of the human spirit. I have faith that no condition is beyond its redemptive power. What matters is the faith and courage to let the spirit take me where it will, to teach me what I need to know in each circumstance of my life.

Now, if only I can remember these things, hold my own preaching close to me. And if memory fails, may I keep something eternal deep in the bone to sustain me. It is this: Above the turbulent waters of anxiety and the restraining levee of reason, the spirit broods.

On Turning Seventy

PHYLLIS B. O'CONNELL

When I was fifty-three a counterperson at McDonald's asked me if I wanted the senior special. "I'm not a senior," I said. "Our senior meals are for those fifty-five and older," she explained. "I'm not fifty-five," I replied, wondering how she could possibly think I was that old since I was still holding out hope that I looked forty-nine.

Today, I regularly ask for senior discounts everywhere I go. I ask because now, a decade and a half later, I really am old. Granted, I am young-old. Still, by anyone's standards, I am certainly well within the category of senior.

I turned seventy this year. I am not happy about it, but I am trying to accept it as I am trying to anticipate so much of what aging will mean for the years ahead.

For the immediate future, I have a plan. I am going to retire this summer. I am in the process of selling my spacious condominium and looking for a much smaller apartment either on or near public transportation.

While I am no stranger to moving or the disorientation moving brings, this move feels particularly momentous. I know I'm approaching it with far more trepidation than previous moves. I wish I could embrace the excitement I want to feel about this new chapter in my life. Sometimes I can, but always lurking around the edges are feelings of uncertainty, anxiety, and occasionally even dread.

On good days I fantasize about having unlimited time for museums, music, plays, travel, family visits, lunch with friends, courses, volunteering, and unencumbered space and time to read and write. What could be better than that? More often, however, I worry. I worry about money and how I'll live on my modest retirement fund. I worry about how I'll do without the safety net of work and the structure it provides, and finally I worry about whether six months or a year into retirement, I will feel as though I am free floating through space wondering if my untethered life has any meaning to me or to anyone else.

Yet, I am trying to keep a sense of balance about the losses and the gains retirement will bring. For the first time in twenty-five years, I will not be a parish minister serving a church. What will that be like?

Will I still be a minister in any real sense? Even now I go to ministers' meetings and feel just a little over the hill. My professional identity isn't everything, but it's a major part of who I am, and I don't want to lose it.

So many unknowns lie ahead, so much to worry about. My single biggest worry about the future is money. If I'm careful, I should be fine until I'm eighty-five, but then what?

Do I join eHarmony hoping for a companionable late marriage? Do I depend on my children? Go back to work? Conveniently die?

I was twenty-four when I interviewed with the human resources director of a large New York publishing company. I remember smiling as he told me that if I worked there until I was sixty-five, I would be a millionaire when I retired. How foolish, I thought, that anyone would imagine I would ever be sixty-five. Looking back, I don't regret not having committed my life to Prentice Hall, but right now I would be more than happy to be retiring with that million dollars.

So, the thing we're never supposed to talk about, money, is sure to be a constant concern.

Then there is time. Will unlimited free days and nights turn out to be a blessing or a curse? I remember once reading a quotation that said, "Millions yearn for immortality yet don't know what to do with themselves on a rainy Sunday afternoon." Is that what retirement will be like: too many rainy Sunday afternoons?

Writer Louisa Thomas says, "Old age is not a country one can visit and leave." I realize that's exactly what I want to do; I want to visit for a little while and see how it goes, and if I don't like it, well, then do something else.

People say seventy is just a number. For me, it's a number that feels like a ninety-degree turn toward a very different life. I think I'll like this new life of walking more and taking public transportation far more often and having easy access to all the places I want to go. No more driving to Symphony Hall only to find the garages full and no on-street parking anywhere.

But this ninety-degree turn also means real compromise. In theory, I am willing to sacrifice space for location, but in reality, I have been looking at apartments so small they would easily fit in my current living room. There's much to be said for downsizing, for de-cluttering, and I'm all for it.

I realize this move will mean giving up much, if not most, of what I now own, from furniture to pictures to cherished sets of china.

While it's easy to scoff at our attachment to material things—a first-world problem if ever there was one—the fact is they are our things and they matter. My things are alive with memories. My grandmother served Thanksgiving dinner on the dishes I'll soon have no room to store. Every wall in my condominium is covered with framed posters and pictures from museums in France and Italy; each one a reminder of an earlier and happier time in a marriage now over. A dining room table that comfortably fits ten, or even twelve if we squeeze together, and has hosted decades of family holiday meals has not a ghost of a chance fitting in a small, very small, studio.

What was it William James said about one's things? "The loss of possessions . . . gives a sense of the shrinkage of our personality; a partial conversion of ourselves to nothingness." His perception is dramatic, to be sure, but the feel is right. We know that aging is synonymous with loss, and this drastic downsizing feels like the first big step in a trove of losses yet to come.

Right now, I envision the next five years as an independent time, which I welcome; yet I also worry whether I will be too much on my own and too alone with too little expected of me. So much of the goodness of life comes from belonging and feeling connected. How do we do that once the children are grown, the marriage is gone, and someone else is sitting at our desk?

And it's not just a sense of connection that brings life's deep satisfactions. Satisfactions also come from feeling we're contributing, that what we do and who we are in the world actually makes a difference.

I wonder if previous generations had such angst about aging. I wish I had asked my grandmother what being old was like, but I was only twelve when she died, and it never occurred to me to ask her what her life was like. She and my grandfather grew old together in the house they had lived in almost their entire marriage. Today there's a name for that: aging in place.

My grandparents just aged without fuss. Sometime in her late seventies, my grandmother had a stroke and died, and my grandfather died six months later. We thought he had died of a broken heart, but the medical diagnosis was lymphoma. There were no ninety-degree turns for my grandparents. They just quietly got old, and now I look back on their lives with a sense of bemusement, and envy too.

In addition to my immediate retirement plan, I also have a midrange and long-range plan, each neatly divided into five-year segments; a little reminiscent of Chairman Mao's Great Leap Forward during the Cold War.

So far, plans two and three only involve reassessing my needs at approximately five-year intervals and making realistic adjustments: maybe a retirement community, a warmer climate, or continuing to live where I happen to be and *age in place*.

The free-floating, nebulous quality of aging, along with the uncertainty that getting old brings, strikes fear into the hearts of people like me, who need to feel they have control over their lives and their futures. With these five-year plans, I know I am attempting the impossible: trying to take hold of my old age and insist that it follow an orderly pattern, insist on some discipline and clarity and predictability. And really, who am I kidding? The unknown factors of retirement alone scare me half to death, never mind the physical changes and conditions of aging, from memory loss to joint replacement surgeries to the ever-increasing possibility of life-threatening illnesses.

The good news is that I am not aging on my own. Most of my friends are all right there with me. They are as old as I am, and we are all facing the same unknowns. And, while aging may be new for us, we need to remember that we are not pioneers on this path. For each of us, the cycle of life comes full circle. Birth, life, and death.

For the immediate future, I expect to be on the go, doing what, I'm not quite sure, but at least in my soon-to-be-on-public-transportation location, I'll be positioned to do it. Then in years that follow I expect to pull back and look for satisfactions closer to home.

Whoever knows what chance, fate, or fortune will bring? And because we don't know, our best bet, always, is to be present to the moment at hand.

Carpe diem, wrote the poet Horace in 23 BCE. It is good advice, especially for those of us who are aging and facing a future that, at best, is only partly in our hands.

For Most This Amazing Life

RICHARD S. GILBERT

E. E. Cummings opens one of his poems with these words: "I thank thee god for most this amazing day." But why stop there? I (as a mystical religious humanist) thank whatever gods there be for most this amazing life. As I experience my eighth decade of existence, I find life all the more amazing, intense, and meaningful despite my inexorable demise. Or perhaps it is because of that inevitable ending of the human project, which greatly concentrates my mind and soul. Perhaps it is because I know my fate that I find life evermore worthwhile. As with the mountaineer, the climb has left me a little short of breath, but I behold a view more entrancing than ever.

Cummings reminds me of writer Annie Dillard's advice to those facing death: say thank you rather than please—offer thanksgiving for the gift of life rather than begging to be spared death's harsh reality. Dillard helps us move from the grim reaper mentality of counting the days we have left to appreciating the days that have been while living fully in the moment. Gratitude always helps us balance our lives, both to take stock of what we *have been* and to remind ourselves that we still *are*. It seems that the quality of life increases even as its span decreases—if we live it with grace and courage. We have not lived a life to end it without meaning. Sometimes a single experience is the cognitive dissonance we need to keep on keeping on.

I saw a T-shirt that immediately caught my attention with its in-your-face wisdom: "Aging is the ultimate extreme sport." Weren't extreme sports activities that have life-and-death risks, like mountain climbing? I thought of those who try to sail around the world solo. I remembered the courage of an amazing woman who swam from Cuba to the United States. These folks deliberately put their lives on the line in the interest of human adventure. And that T-shirt, worn by a colleague about my age, came back into focus. I've risked arrest in protests; I've skied on some rather scary slopes; I've even tried a rock-climbing wall, but nothing quite compares with the ultimate extreme sport of aging.

That T-shirt is good for a laugh—or a good cry—
or some deep meditation. Athletes of the spirit find
in the aging process quite enough adventure to
challenge and satisfy the soul.

Aging does not so much require the physical
courage of civil disobedience or high climbing or
dangerous sailing or swimming with jellyfish. It
requires spiritual courage, the courage to acknowledge that the causes we have served throughout our
career have not yet come to fruition, and won't during
our lifetime; that the dreams of youthful idealism
are not going to be fulfilled; and that we have to
learn to live with it.

It requires the spiritual courage to yield lead-
ership to younger colleagues who may do it differ-
ently.

It requires the spiritual courage to face up to
our limitations and not feel self-pity; to bid a fond
farewell to good friends; to lose a loved one and
keep living life to the full even when lonely.

It requires the spiritual courage to realize that
we will not live to see how the lives of our children
and grandchildren fully unfold.

It requires the spiritual courage to know that,
after all, life is terminal—even the good life we
have tried to lead.

Sometimes those transformative and teaching experiences come from the young. My wife and I do a fair amount of child care with our grandchildren. A 6:00 a.m. phone call more often than not brings news of a sick grandchild (we have three in town—ages five, seven, and eleven). We enjoy being helpful, and we get to know our grandchildren as well; that is one reason we remain in the city where we have lived for more than forty years.

Moreover, this responsibility is a learning opportunity. Take, for example, what I have learned from our eleven-year-old grandson, Sam. We had taken all three to a library playground after school. I was playing tag with them, rather unsuccessfully chasing them around. Of course, I was always "it." Other children on the playground joined in the fun. One of them shouted a warning to Sam: "Watch out, he (referring to me) will catch you!" Sam stood there, a few feet from me, smiling, arms confidently crossed, and said, "He's my grandfather. I can easily outrun him!"

And, of course, he was right. A seventy-something with arthritis is no match for an athletic eleven-year-old boy. That didn't make it any easier to take, however. I fancied myself an athlete in my younger days—football, basketball, baseball, tennis, skiing, and so on. I didn't know quite how to respond—with an embarrassed admission that he was right or with pride in the athletic prowess of a boy who has some of my genes.

So it goes that our grandchildren teach us to age gracefully. My increasing limitations are balanced by my pride and joy in their increasing capacity. I'm coming to admit that I just can't do what I used to do, though I have stubbornly fought to do so. I hope they appreciate that I try to keep up. And I try to stay in shape—if only to enjoy long hikes, brisk swims, and hide-and-seek with them.

I find it a challenge to age gracefully, but try I must. It helps to remember that I was once like that eleven-year-old grandson. It helps to remember how grateful I have been to enjoy the sheer bodily energy of sports. And it helps to be grateful for what has been, and for the generations unfolding before my appreciative eyes. Growing older is not for wimps, that's for sure. There are compensations, however. And one of them is a red-haired grandson who knows he can easily outrun me.

I was born on September 21, a cusp, the boundary between summer and fall. That image of being on a boundary is fitting for elders. We are between end of career and end of life, a space that can be miserable or meaningful depending on how we deal with *retirement*, an unfortunate term. We may be retired from earning a living, but we have not retired from living a life, setting the past in proper context, anticipating a future, and digging deeply into both the past and the present for meaning.

James Russell Lowell visited Ralph Waldo Emerson on the latter's seventieth birthday and called it an "auspicious occasion." "On the contrary," replied Emerson, "it is a melancholy one." "What do you mean?" asked Lowell. Emerson explained, "It means the end of youth."

I agree. Being well past that marker, I find myself in an ambivalent position—carefully tightrope walking between retirement and career, nostalgia and commitment, reflection and action, life and death.

Which way to lean? I still want to participate fully in the action and passion of the times, as Oliver Wendell Holmes called it. I am passionately engaged in peace and justice work; I enjoy being a grandfather; I relish being with my family more frequently; I enjoy watching a football game without guilt that I should be working on a sermon. I have books I want to write and trips I want to take. My time is limited. There is so much more I want to do—and to be.

At the same time I enjoy looking back on my life. To help celebrate our fiftieth wedding anniversary I created a PowerPoint program from my spouse's and my earliest days to the present. What a hoot! Red-haired, brush-cut, newly minted minister marries beautiful fellow Universalist. It was a trip down memory lane.

And I devote time to an ongoing project— saving onto a thumb drive digitized files of my sermons, talks, and writings from over a half century of ministry. This involves scanning, a little retyping, and a bit of nostalgic reading of old sermons. They're not as bad as I thought they might be. My plan is to give the thumb drive to my sons. I'm not sure they will spend hours reading my sermons and writings, but something in me needs to sum up my career tangibly. Perhaps this thumb drive is physical evidence that I have really lived.

A thumb drive. Is that all there is to capture my life? Probably not, but the words of ministry reflect deeds done, experiences lived, people served. They trace a history, both of soul and of society—of life lived in a larger context. My thumb drive becomes a kind of ethical will and testament.

Wallowing in the past at the expense of the present can be dangerous. At the same time, being so busy with *now* that we have little time to reflect on *then* has its risks. So I experience this creative tension—a healthy tension, I think—between reflecting on the meaning of what has been and acting in the present for the future. My thumb drive is a work in progress. It both embraces my past and invites my future. Thank goodness space is not an issue!

In addition to my ministerial life, I have precious memories from daily life with loved ones. I deposit the sights and sounds of these experiences in my memory bank. They are what poet Wallace Stevens calls "moments of inherent excellence," and they sustain me as I realize that these moments will not go on forever. On the other hand, such moments can never be taken from me or from those with whom I shared them. They reside safely in all our memory banks.

One of these moments involved three generations of Gilberts surrounding a beautiful but old ping-pong hockey box. Berea College students built it more than forty years ago, and it has been a regular presence at our holiday family gatherings. This rectangular wooden box contains six wooden dowels, three light and three dark, with one, two, or three paddles to emulate a hockey team. A ping-pong ball serves as the puck. Each year the games become a bit more competitive as our grandchildren are more physically able and have inhaled some of the family competitiveness.

I can still picture the most recent game: our older son fiercely battling to bang that innocent ping-pong ball into the goal, past the single wooden stick stubbornly manipulated by our younger son; our eleven-year-old grandson quickly adapting to the fun as he delightedly scored on his grandfather; our seven-year-old grandson trying to defend against father and uncle; and finally, our five-year-old granddaughter trying to keep up her end of this intense game. Grandma wisely kept out of the scrum by keeping score, while our daughter-in-law enjoyed the raucous verbal mayhem from the kitchen.

I can't for the life of me remember who won— as if that mattered. We all won, judging by the ohs and ahs and the oh nos, and other exclamations of success or failure. By the time the game ended we were all ready to eat around a single table. We have a small family and are able to be together at the high holy days of the year. In that we are fortunate.

I'm not such a captive of nostalgia that I don't count on a good many more such times. I relish them and only hope the others do as well. Having shared so many memorial services with so many people, I know how precious they are. When people come to remember loved ones, it is these withdrawals from the memory bank that come to mind—and heart and voice—in laughter and in tears.

That is my banking theory of aging. I joyfully deposit as much as I can; I joyfully withdraw as much as I need.

We have only one life cycle to live. At times I feel that one is not quite enough. In my more exuberant moments I would love to have several bites of the apple. But when I come back to reality, I realize the unique life that is mine will have to be lived in one segment. All the meaning that was and is and is to be will have to be contained in this one-and-only life cycle.

As one wit put it, "We're all just penciled in." Of course, this is right. We need to remind ourselves we are finite creatures in a vast reality. On the other hand, we are the creatures who understand that and are grateful we have been privileged to make our mark. Thanks be for most this amazing life!

Being Still

JUDITH MEYER

I retired at fifty-nine because I needed to turn my attention to caring for my family. My husband was diagnosed with Parkinson's disease shortly after my father died from the same illness. My mother-in-law, who had been living independently well into her nineties, entered a swift decline. We were called home—to my husband's hometown. In a short time I said good-bye to my congregation, sold our home, moved across the country, renovated our new home, attended to my mother-in-law in the last year of her life, officiated at her burial, and then tried to understand what came next.

In less than two years I had relinquished work that largely defined who I was and found myself in a community where people knew me only through my connection to my husband and his family. My new work, which included at times caregiver and general contractor, gave me plenty to do, but did not provide me with an identity. I didn't know how to express myself as the person I had become.

Learning to appreciate what this experience has taught me has taken several years. Retirement is a developmental task. It comes with change and loss and requires us to adjust in every aspect of our life. Everything we do from here on is done against the backdrop of the inevitability of death and the constant presence of grieving.

Given this reality, this time of life could be a joyless contraction of the self to the point of no return. Or it could be something else: the fulfillment of radically altered goals and an invitation to live in the present. I have been contemplating these alternatives over the past few years.

I have found myself looking back at my life, noting that formative events and relationships were not necessarily as I would have expected them. The things I have loved since I was a child—music, church, animals—have made me who I am as much as my work has. I feel gratitude toward the women's movement and its positive life-changing effects. Turning points in my life have consisted of times when I had the courage to make an adventurous move or fall in love; when I had struggled through confusion and anxiety to make a significant personal step forward.

Defining myself in these terms has brought me back to my original gifts and values and has allowed me to make happy choices about how to spend my time. I have become a musician again, studying the piano. There is something about immersing myself in learning new music, reacquainting myself with the person who once did this with complete concentration, that is expansive and joyful. I never realized how much I missed it and how much pleasure it gives me.

I go to church. I walk my dog. I still care about women's issues, perhaps more than ever.

My work is to stay in the present moment. It's difficult for someone like me. I am driven by anxiety, always planning ahead, trying to cover every possibility. This quality makes me a good caregiver and traveler, but it is not the best strategy for aging or facing mortality. Staying in the present is the best strategy.

Right now my husband does not need me as a full-time caregiver. He is vital and busy with his own work. Who knows what the future will bring? At this time he and I are paying attention to life. We are still learning. And I am learning to be still.

Possessed

PETER MORALES

Once in a while, usually late in the evening, I listen to one of Beethoven's late quartets. I can't listen to them often. They are simply too intense. They are certainly *not* background music.

Something happened to, or more likely within, Beethoven as he grew older. His music remained ruggedly beautiful, but he longer was trying to prove himself. The struggle had changed, become more internal. He charged ahead less and reflected more.

I almost never look at the late art of Francisco Goya. It is too disturbing, too dark. The successful court painter who created portraits for Spanish royalty became a man who shoves before us frightening visions of evil and madness.

I am neither Beethoven nor Goya. Yet, as I come to terms with senior discounts, cranky joints, and I look ahead to not being employed for the first time since junior high school, I want to learn their lessons. They were able to let go of what made them "successful" and surrender to new visions, new sounds, new possibilities.

My life didn't go as I planned—not even close. Looking back, I'm glad; for the life I have led has been a much richer adventure than the one I planned. Ironically, although my life did not go as I planned, I *chose* the life I led.

What in heaven possessed me to get on a bus that hot August evening in San Antonio and ride for two days to Stockton, California? I was seventeen years old. I had been outside Texas only once. I was lured by a college catalog to a new experimental college modeled largely on Oxford and Cambridge. Small classes. Seminars. Intense interaction in an idealistic learning community. Crazy kids in the 1960s.

I had a vague sense that this choice would change everything, and it did. I experienced an intellectual big bang—anthropology, humanism, Spanish literature, physics, the social sciences, philosophy, intellectual history. I lost my religion. I fell in love with Phyllis, who would share my life. Getting on that bus changed everything. What possessed me?

And what in heaven possessed us, in our late thirties, to quit good jobs, cash in our retirement savings, sell our home, and buy a struggling community newspaper in Oregon? That was beyond risky; it was *crazy*. And what a wonderful experience those eleven years in journalism turned out to be. It was community ministry before I had ever heard the term. We met fascinating people. I could see my work make a difference. I loved framing the news and writing preachy editorials. Oh, and we joined a Unitarian Universalist congregation in Eugene, Oregon.

I got to thinking secretly about ministry. Finally I got up the courage to say so out loud. To my surprise, Phyllis had also been thinking about ministry being a path for me. So, just shy of my fiftieth birthday, we sold our home, dropped everything, and went to Starr King School for the Ministry in Berkeley. Once again, the lure of committed, idealistic community lured us on. This was risky, especially at my age. I went on to serve Jefferson Unitarian Church in Golden, Colorado. Parish ministry was the most satisfying and rewarding work I had ever done.

The last great risky decision came when I decided to become a candidate for president of the Unitarian Universalist Association. I began as a clear underdog. The most likely outcome was not only losing the election but also having to leave one of the best ministerial settlements in our association. What possessed me? Something deep inside propelled me. Being elected UUA president has turned out to be the greatest challenge of all, with the highest stakes.

Looking back, it all appears so inevitable. But each of the big choices was made after months—and sometimes years—of doubt and uncertainty. Each big change was frightening. Each involved huge risk.

I see now that what lured me on to the bus in San Antonio is what lured me to community journalism and to ministry. I see, too, that each time I chose not to pursue some new challenge, each time I opted for safety and financial security, I was miserable.

What possessed me? I was driven, I now see, not just by idealism but also by a need to act, to do something significant. Maybe I also needed to prove something to myself. Lord knows, I pushed myself.

I am not Beethoven, but I have lived the struggles of the *Appassionata* sonata and the Fifth Symphony. Soon enough those struggles will end.

If health holds, I will retire in three years at age seventy. One day I am president of the UUA and, suddenly, the next day, I enter a great unknown—a blank.

Can I surrender to that emptiness? Can I learn to wait rather than act? Can I learn to be an elder? Do I have it in me to be still? Can I be at peace rather than preach about it? This may be the greatest challenge yet.

Perhaps I should listen to the slow movement of Beethoven's Opus 135 quartet.

I have lived possessed. What, I wonder, is it like to have nothing to prove? What, I wonder, will I allow to possess me then?

Recently Retired

KATE TUCKER

It's delicious to ditch the alarm clock. Most days, now, I can. No more buzzer, no more throwing off the blankets to get to the coffee, to get to the day's list. No more jumping up before I notice whether I'm alive. Now, when I wake, I wake slowly, like a submarine surfacing.

Once I know I'm back and breathing, my mind goes looking for my arms and legs. There they are. All are calm. In fact, all are stone. Gravity has me. I'm a marble effigy lying on one of those tombs in Westminster Abbey, arms folded forever. I can't lift any part, even to remove a foam earplug.

I want to accept the gift of being unhurried, so for a while I honor inertia and lie there following wisps of dreams. Where did they take me last night? To which rooms, with which siblings, neighbors, film actors, congregants? This morning

I can only recall being with a college roommate, searching city streets for a car we parked somewhere. Most mornings deliver souvenirs from the deep. They aren't always dreams. They take many forms. I hoped this would happen. I hoped that getting older would bring this around.

I have a 1995 audiotape of a National Public Radio interview with the late writer and editor William Maxwell. He was far into his eighties when he spoke with NPR's Linda Wertheimer. I keep an old tape player just so I can listen to him.

In one of the gentlest voices I've ever heard, Maxwell says that being old is the most interesting thing that's ever happened to him, because, he says, with old age comes "the opening of memory." He says the past comes closer than ever, and flows into the present with bewildering ease. He describes an experience he had in the night, in bed, in which he was suddenly able to remember in detail the house he grew up in. He could go room to room and examine things he hadn't seen for more than seventy years—pictures, books, furniture—and he could look at them as long as he wanted to. "It was as if some shutter had slipped back in my mind and I had absolute, total memory of the past. And when I had enough I just willingly let go of it. It was a marvelous experience," he says, "and it makes me believe that everything is there, absolutely everything. The whole of our life is accessible at the moment when we're open to it."

This intrigues me. What will float up from the sea of memory, and when? And why? Whoever it is down there—or in there—gathering, mixing, revealing, I trust her. I trust her industriousness, her aim, and her timing.

A month ago I woke with one short line of a children's song looping in my head—a line utterly familiar and completely surprising, since it hadn't come to mind for well over six decades. I phoned my Michigan brother and sang the looping line, which goes, "Won't you ever grow up, Little Toot?"

"Does that ring a bell, Kev?" I asked. "Did we have a record or something? Who was Little Toot?" Kevin thought. He said, "Yes, I can see the record, a yellow forty-five with a blue center. Toot was a tugboat. There must've been a book as well, because I remember pictures. If I recall, Toot raced around the harbor making waves and bothering other boats, till he finally did something heroic—maybe rescued a ship in a storm."

I didn't remember Toot racing around the harbor, but I remembered Kevin and me racing around the haven of our living room, romping to the music on our records—galloping to "The Big Rock Candy Mountain" and skipping to Danny Kaye's version of "The Emperor's New Clothes." Dancing, dancing, we circled the coffee table until (as Mom later said) we wore a trench in the carpet. It's a wonder to be in the body that way. This body, which wasn't built to last. While it's here and strong, may I still answer to the music. This is a prayer.

I enjoy the fact that Little Toot showed up the morning after I agreed to write a personal essay (this one) on aging. "Won't you ever grow up, Little Toot?" At age three, was this my introduction to the challenge of moving through time? Will you grow up? *Up*, of course, means nothing now. Up is for those who are short due to being young. But growth remains a shining possibility, and aging is simply the gift of continuing on.

I mentioned this in a phone talk with Kathy, my first friend from kindergarten days. I told her how Little Toot came out of nowhere. She understood. She said, "I just had a memory pop up that way." Then she told me about a moment she hasn't thought of since it happened, back on the farm, when she was eleven or twelve.

Her father, a gruff and loving man, was down in the well, mending the walls. He asked Kathy to lower a bucket of bricks into the well. She started, she slipped, the bucket dropped, and when she heard it hit she began crying and howling apologies, knowing her father's temper and not knowing if she'd killed him. But then, when her dad put his head up out of the well—and this is what stunned and saved her—he had a merry gleam in his eye. He was laughing. Now, at age sixty-seven, the scene comes back to her, along with the surprise and relief, which makes her cry again.

I'm not one to volunteer unsolicited interpretations or projections, so I didn't, but I couldn't help sensing the genius in that memory. You see, at the time of our phone talk, Kathy—a woman always upright and energetic—was sitting, foot up, with a recently and severely broken leg. As the oldest child, Kathy had said, when her dying father asked her to look out for her mother, "Of course, gladly." And gladly she's done it, all through her mother's fifteen years of Alzheimer's disease. These past several years, her mother has lived in a care facility, and Kathy has been there with almost daily visits, hair brushing, hand massages, and always, on leaving, a quiet recitation of the Lord's Prayer. She's been there, that is, until recently, when her femur snapped like a pretzel and she couldn't leave her house or even her sofa. And then (as I imagine it), before any cloud of guilt could form in her, this memory intervened, bringing her a vision of her beaming father, the face of reassurance—as if to say, "Be at rest. No harm done, my darling."

Surprises from the past are just one part of this new chapter, a chapter that feels as distinctive as the onset of adolescence. I discuss this with others who are in their sixties. When we exit the years of intense service—whether parenting or the production line or the professions (in my case, parish ministry)—time feels different. The lives we chose came with structures and schedules not of our choosing. Now, minus the imperatives and deadlines, the present moment expands, even as the Big Deadline comes closer. In the days ahead, we don't necessarily want old habits to rule. Psychiatrist Carl Jung said, "What is a normal goal to a young person becomes a neurotic hindrance in old age." This makes good, solid sense to me. So this becomes a time of watching, of listening, of discernment.

Which I suppose is the reason I linger between waking and rising. I want to notice the subtleties. I want to take the opportunity to wait and wonder, Which promise or anticipation or inspiration will bring me to my feet this morning? Which thought will cause me to challenge gravity and rise? It's really a question about effort. Effort: "a conscious exertion of power." Lately, I'm keen on the word itself. Effort used to mean one thing, back when I rose from sleep tethered to assignments and commitments. But now? What will effort come to mean in this more spacious time? Maybe it will feel less like pushing or pulling, and more like simply not wanting to miss a chance to be faithful.

What will constitute effort now? It's a simple question with a simple answer, but it took an echocardiogram to remind me. My doctor ordered it, so I went to the clinic and reclined while a sonographer performed the ultrasound procedure that transmits a picture of the heart in motion. The somewhat ghostly image appeared on a screen, and I watched.

I'd never seen my heart before. There it was, the little pump that's kept me alive through the barely conscious years, the rigorous years, the searching years, and the finding. Through the awful aching and the joyful leaping. There it was, with its delicate quartet of valves fluttering a hundred thousand times a day, busy valves that have charming names (mitral, tricuspid, aortic, pulmonic) and that, after all these years, still pulse in tempo: "Sustain, sustain, sustain,

sustain." I was overtaken by reverence for a muscle. I addressed my thanks to the image on the screen. "Thank you. Bless you. How steadfast you are."

"The heart is a leisurely muscle," wrote David Steindl-Rast, a Benedictine monk. This seems to be true. We don't exert conscious effort to make the heart work. Electrical signals take care of it. If possible, I'd like future effort to be more like that. Move the way the heart moves. Be a leisurely, loyal, songful muscle. Let the pulses of energy or light decide everything. Mornings, I can put the question directly to the little pump: "What shall we do today? Where you say to go, that's where I'll go."

I'm talking about attending to the motions of love. It's not just my heart. Every heart is a veiled hero, and that's the whole of my catechism. What's clear now is that, in the end, what will matter is not how well or poorly I perform in this life, but how much of the world I let in.

This morning it's enough to lie inert for a while, scanning the earth and its continents, imagining all the ones who rise from sleep: the forest dwellers in their huts, the fishermen in their harbor villages, the dementia patients in their double rooms, the bus drivers in Chicago, the camel drivers of the Sahara, the schoolchildren of Belize, the prisoners in their cells, the nursing mothers everywhere. All who sleep and rise, including the chickens in their backyard coops.

It's enough to lie here awhile in a state of thanks. Thanks for family and friends, each one. Thanks for this good mattress and for the eggs waiting in the fridge. Thanks for this meeting of memory and possibility and for the appetite to embark, to rise and go and be changed yet again. One day my legs won't carry me, but that day hasn't come.

When my stone eyelids crack open, I see pencils of light around the door frame. It feels like 7:00 a.m. It feels like Tuesday, and it is. Today, what brings me to my feet is Colleen's Total Fitness class. There's still time to get there.

In Colleen's class, I'm probably the oldest of the exercisers. We're a comfortable group. By now we know each other's family challenges, vacation schedules, and T-shirt wardrobes. Three mornings a week, for a full hour, we're one in spirit, united in our determination to be supple and ready for what life brings. We shed our coats, take our places, and, following beautiful Colleen, we reach and kick and lunge and lift, while the Bee Gees sing, "You should be dancing, yeah" and the Pointer Sisters sing, "Jump, jump for my love."

Lesson from Great Pond

GARY E. SMITH

When my mother died, she was eighty-nine years old; she wanted with all her heart to live even longer, but she could not. At her memorial service, I said that she was, for a long time, my one and only personal archivist, collecting every sermon I ever wrote, both in print and on tape, a vast library that I said would be worth nothing some day. And how I longed for her to say, "Gary, that was a terrible sermon last Sunday. I just don't think you were up to it." But she never did.

At her memorial service, my brother read from E. B. White's essay "Once More to the Lake," which is about a lake in Maine where my brother lives now. White tells of a place our family knows, Bear Spring Camps, on the north end of the lake and of the waitresses there. "The same country girls [each year]," White says, "there having been no passage of

time, only the illusion of it as in a dropped curtain—
the waitresses were still fifteen . . . [a] pattern of life
indelible, the fade proof lake, the woods unshatter-
able, the pasture with the sweet fern and the juni-
per forever and ever, summer without end."

My mother was one of those country-girl waitresses that White saw and wrote about, my brother
said. She worked at Bear Springs during her high
school summers. We have a picture of her, with
the other girls, posing on the broad front steps
of the farmhouse. She has a cooking pot on her
head. Three generations have now worked there:
my mother, my brother, my niece. White was right:
"No passage of time, only the illusion."

I have two brothers, an older brother who lives
in West Virginia and this brother who lives on Great
Pond. We are rarely together, but in early October,
three years before she died, we were together, my
mother, brothers, and me. All the leaves had not
yet turned, the sun still had warmth, the sky was so
blue, and the four of us went out in a boat, out into
the lake, an easy trip with no destination, following
first this loon and then that one, taking pictures,
talking, and laughing.

I was aware then that all kinds of complicated
relationships were in that boat on that afternoon.

There are complicated relationships in all families, but I was so blessed that day, for I was aware of letting it all go for the moment, letting it go, not trying to analyze it, not trying to make a speech (or a sermon) about it, not being maudlin about it, simply going into that moment and finding myself awash in gratitude. Here I am in a boat in the middle of the lake with my brothers and my mother, with the sun and the water and the wind and the colors and the beauty and the peace.

The author Tom Robbins writes,

Perhaps a person gains by accumulating obstacles. Care must be taken, however, to select large obstacles, for only those of sufficient scope and scale have the capacity to lift us out of context and force life to appear in an entirely new and unexpected light. For example, should you litter the floor and tabletops of your room with small objects . . . you step around the objects, pick them up, knock them aside. Should you, on the other hand, encounter in your room a nine thousand pound granite boulder, the surprise it evokes, the extreme steps that must be taken to deal with it, compel you to see with

105

new eyes. Difficulties illuminate existence,
but they must be fresh and of high quality.

I am remembering now an event in my early
ministry, a moment I had long forgotten, for the
sheer "nine-thousand-pound boulder" of it all.
Here I am, in a parking lot near Mount Marcy in
the Adirondacks, with a youth group from Connecticut. And we have been hiking and camping all
the weekend long, and it is Monday of Memorial
Day weekend and now we can go home, and I can
shower, and I can be in my own home, and I can
sleep, and I can stop counting teenagers.

And my car will not start, and did I mention
that it is raining, and that my car is in a remote
parking lot, and that it is Memorial Day weekend,
and that tow truck people are effectively ignoring
me on the other end of the non-cell phone line.
Please imagine me there, at my twenty-six-year-old
immature worst, sitting in a dead car because of the
rain, sitting with five overtired teenage people, sitting there with all the other drivers and chaperones
and teenagers in their own cars, because they will
not leave without me.

And there comes a tap at my extremely
fogged-up window, and I wind the window down

to find one of the chaperones there, draped in a dripping bright pink poncho. She says to me, dirty and unshaven, impatient and near tears, she says to me, "Praise the Lord!" And she smiles and turns on her heel and returns to her car. There is a stunned silence in my car. I am being asked to pay attention. Her words are a blessing. The tow truck comes. My car is repaired. We go home.

Could it have been that the rain, the dead battery, the grubbiness, the desperation, the pink poncho, the directive, could it have been that all this was one nine-thousand-pound granite boulder, and I still could not see it? "Difficulties illuminate existence," says Tom Robbins. "But they must be fresh and of high quality." *Praise the Lord*, by any other name, is an invitation to pay attention.

I continue to learn that this life we have been given to lead has twists and turns we can never imagine, has joys and sorrows plenty, has disappointments and surprises, has triumphs and tragedies over which we have no control. What takes our measure, it seems to me, is our own discernment. Shall we take notice? Shall we praise? Shall we be grateful? This is what aging has brought me and taught me.

In my nearly forty years of ministry I have had the great privilege and honor of peeking into so many lives and of knowing the nine-thousand-pound granite boulders that filled room after room. I am in awe of the great courage, dexterity, and tenacity so many people brought to their lives when dealing with outrageous obstacles that often blocked their way. I had a front-row seat for all of this.

What have I learned? I have learned to embrace those I love and those who love me, and to speak a silent prayer. I have learned that my own life holds its share of complicated relationships, and like that October day on the lake, I can be attentive: to feel the wind, hear the laughter, see the golden leaves, over and over and over again. I have learned to be attentive. I have learned to be grateful.

The Small Stuff

DENISE TAFT DAVIDOFF

I have had three bouts of cancer, and the experiences have increased my belief that it is folly to sweat the small stuff. My manicurist muffed an appointment earlier today and apologized with great remorse—again and again and again—as if to justify her having accidentally cut off one of my fingers. Big deal. I had to wait twenty minutes. Finally, I pointed to the skin graft on the top of my head and told her I was feeling celebratory today because my hair had grown in sufficiently so I did not feel the need to wear a hat. I didn't care that I had to wait to get my nails done. Perspective.

My first breast cancer was discovered in August 1985 when I was fifty-three. I had a lumpectomy, and the tumor was such that, two days later, I went back to the hospital for removal of the lymph nodes under my left armpit. Only one indicated spread.

My doctors—gynecologist, internist, oncologist, surgeon—were divided about the need for chemotherapy. Two were for it, but two were against it, saying that the chance of further spread was minimal. "You have now officially gone through the looking glass," my internist told me. "You need to weigh the choices and make up your own mind." For me, it was a no-brainer. Why would I want to wake up five or ten years later and say, "Oh, hell, I should have done the chemo." My dear husband and sons concurred. But, if they hadn't, I would have done chemo anyway. When you have cancer, you need to do everything you can to save your own life.

A few years ago, in February 2012, a mammogram indicated the possibility of cancer in the right breast. At eighty-one, my response was different than at fifty-three. In 1985 I wanted to keep on living. In 2012 I wanted to keep on living, but I was also acutely aware of gratitude for the splendid life I had already lived. Luckily, following lumpectomy and radiation, the doctors proclaimed clean margins, and I was back on the long-life track, feeling blessed and, in truth, a bit smug.

In mid-October of 2013 I felt a growth on the top of my head and went to my dermatologist, who grimly told me it looked like a melanoma. On November 6 (one remembers these dates) he called me to say the lab at Yale New Haven Hospital reported a melanoma, a deep melanoma. "You will need surgery and don't delay." This time, I was very scared. My only brother died of melanoma in 1971, six weeks past his forty-second birthday. Waiting seven weeks for the surgery, I handled my fright by losing myself in work. The ability to emotionally compartmentalize is among humanity's great gifts. I worked well and I slept fitfully. I saw my four grandchildren and their parents. I read poetry and I prayed to a God I cannot describe. And, when it was over, the benediction was once again "No spread and the margins are clean."

Life is precious and I do not sweat the small stuff. And the definition of *small* is getting larger every day.

I am one of the lucky people. I have retained the intellectual capacity for productive thought, the energy for meaningful work, and the reputation and network that provide outlets for my skills and talents on both a paid and a volunteer basis. At this stage of my life, I have the luxury to choose assignments that align with my Unitarian Universalist values and my liberal political views. It is rare for me to awaken to a new day with anything resembling fear or dread. Mostly I bound out of bed—well, *bounding* in the metaphorical sense, since my knees tend to stiffen during the night—eager to get on with whatever is on the list I left on my desk the night before.

What do I worry about? Running out of time. Becoming feeble and dependent. Having to give up driving my car. The stock market crashing. Outliving a child or grandchild.

What do I not worry about (at least not obsessively)? Wrinkles and dry skin. Blemishes on my face. Flabby neck. Past mistakes. Lost loves. Bad and irretrievable financial investments.

I try really hard to live in the present, and mostly I succeed. I cannot do anything about the past and I have little control over the future. So I am impelled to make each day count by keeping promises, helping others, finding ways to be generous, being a friend, practicing awe, counting my blessings.

I am a privileged white citizen in a privileged country, and I try to remember at all times, including the tough times, that I am way, way, way ahead of most of the world's people. My problems are other folks' aspirations. I hope to take this attitude into the challenges I will face as I age. I may have to give up elements of lifestyle that others have never had to begin with. If I'm not able to drive my car, I will have money for taxis and friends to ask for rides. If I need physical therapy in the future, I live in a retirement community with a staff of physical therapists. My aging process is buttressed with gifts and blessings. I try not to sweat the small stuff.

A Song in the Face of Death

JOHN CUMMINS

Blossoms and branches green to coffins all I bring,
For fresh as the morning, thus would I chant a song
for you, O sane and sacred death.

WALT WHITMAN

April is a crazy lady, and I both love her and hate her!
Annually she comes dancing down this hill of spring,
a half-mad pagan grin on her face and flowers in her
hair. Beneath her wild and heathen dance, the crocus
and yellow jonquils spring and everywhere, *everywhere*
green; the green laughter of spring bursting through
the cracks of sidewalks, heaving the concrete, mock-
ing its thin overlay of pretension and organization.
Cast aside with careless abandon are the gloomy cli-
chés of robed priests, their solemn pronouncements
and all presumption of human control. She is entic-
ing, delightful, irresistible, inevitable.

And yet! Beneath the warmth of her touch there lurks an icy wind that often blights the young bud and kills without warning. Behind her madcap grin, deep in her eyes the cruel indifference of the ruthless murderer. The flowers she carries with such reckless abandon filled with hidden thorns and amidst their sweet, seductive perfume, the stench of rotting death. Embrace her, touch her anywhere, and you will come away wounded and bleeding.

"April is the cruelest month," writes T. S. Eliot. In her poem "Spring," Edna St. Vincent Millay says in bitter irony,

> To what purpose, April, do you return again?
> Beauty is not enough.
> You can no longer quiet me with the redness
> Of little leaves opening stickily.
> I know what I know.
> The sun is hot on my neck as I observe
> The spikes of the crocus.
> The smell of the earth is good.
> But . . .
> It is not enough that yearly, down this hill,
> April
> Comes like an idiot, babbling and strewing
>   flowers.

Perhaps because both my father and my son died in this month of April, I am more acutely aware than most that in the midst of life is death; that life, like April, pours forth around us an incredible fountain of indiscriminate beauty, and at the same time tears from us our dearest loves and most tender relationships. The coming of spring does not banish the fact of death. My father died easily, his hand in mine, my name the last word on his lips. I emerged without him into the warmth and sunlight of spring. Voices of children wafted on the warm air. Overhead the sky was blue, and puffy white clouds rolled on as they have ten thousand years before.

I do not believe in a hereafter; nor, for that matter, do I believe in a heretofore! I do believe that each person is a completely unique, one-time, never-before-and-never-again event and that each individual has a contribution to make that is, and forever will be, part of the human story. Even the babe who has lived but five minutes has touched the lives of a dozen others whose lives were forever changed thereby.

Each of us in our lifetime climbs the mountain of human experience—our own and that of our race. When we reach the heights and see what is to be seen, we lie down on that mountain of human experience. The small measure of our dust adds to its height, whereby our peers and companions and those who come after us may see a small way farther than we. And that immortality! No soul that ever lived, however brief or however dim, is without its significance in the ongoing life of the universe.

Our faults and weaknesses, and we all have them, die with us; but our victories of character and spirit remain to bless all humanity forever. For if what a person has done is good, and if what a person has said is true, then that goodness and truth remain to bless all humanity forever. While evil destroys itself, true goodness cannot be killed. The poet John Keats put it this way:

A thing of beauty is a joy forever:
. . . It will never
Pass into nothingness; but will keep
A bower quiet for us, and a sleep
Full of sweet dreams, and health, and quiet
    breathing.
Therefore, on every morrow, are we wreathing
A flowery band to bind us to the earth.

And so, as I now stand in my eighty-eighth year, at death's door, I offer this, my song in the face of death:

Come, my brothers, Come my sisters!
A song let us sing, a song in the face of death —
Hail clouds, hail sky, hail years, hail death!
Past all endings, past all beginnings —
Hail the greening earth!
Star-fire of nameless reaching,
Star-fire of endless reaching
Through cell and seed and birth
Calls a soft and silent mirth —
The time for singing has come,
The flowers appear on the earth!

Exit Strategies

SUSAN WESTON

When I retired a few years ago, I joined the Life-long Learning Collaborative, a large group of retirees engaged in member-taught courses. The collaborative numbers about four hundred, ranging in age from mid-sixties to mid-nineties. The guys tend to be retired doctors, lawyers, and engineers; the women are mostly retired social workers, librarians, and English teachers. The group offers lots of literature and history courses, as well as courses taking advantage of the vibrant cultural arts scene here in Providence, Rhode Island. My first course was a theater class that the coordinators (a retired engineer and a retired nurse) had planned around the city's local productions; we read the plays, attended rehearsals, met directors and actors, wrote mock reviews for the *Providence Journal*, and discussed everything from symbolism in the text to directorial interpretations. I loved every minute of it.

Next I signed up for a contemporary poetry class—not to write, mind you, but to read. I haven't made time to read poetry since I was a graduate student, and here we were, ten or twelve of us spending thirty, forty, sometimes fifty minutes on a single poem. I remarked to a classmate that I felt like I was back in graduate school. But not really. These discussions had nothing competitive about them, no intellectual preening for a professor, none of the academic ambitions that color so much of graduate school. No, the similarity was in what had drawn me to graduate school in the first place: a love of reading. Close reading of nuanced, multi-dimensional texts.

As I left class one day, one of my classmates—a retired lawyer enjoying literature for the first time—said, "Isn't this great?" "Oh, isn't it!" I responded joyously. "I feel returned to myself!"

In my older classmates I am seeing possible futures for myself. When will I need a cane, a walker, assistance getting up from a chair? Already I prefer not to drive at night; one day I will not be able to drive at all, and like ninety-two-year-old Carl, I will stop coming to class unless someone can pick me up. Lyn has had a stroke that has left her looking like a living Cézanne portrait, speaking out of the slipped planes of her face. Her partner, Edith, has dropped out—temporarily, of course—while she has radiation treatment for her cancer. The tremor of Dan's Parkinson's disease agitates his Xerox copy of the poem. Natalie doesn't come to class when it's at all icy; she's afraid of falling. Class discussions are different when she's absent; unlike me, she doesn't hesitate to tell overinterpreters that not *every* detail in a poem has to be meaningful. (There, too, is another possible future: me as an outspoken old crone.)

Perhaps it is this broader involvement with aging people that reignited my interest in end-of-life issues. God knows it's a hot topic these days. Hardly a week goes by without some book or article describing the difficult death of someone's aged parent or the launch of yet another website full of helpful tips for end-of-life planning and how to avoid spending your last six weeks in the intensive care unit. Like a terrier with a chew toy, I have found myself persistently worrying the topic: clipping articles, amassing books, compiling resources.

Using my association with the Lifelong Learning Collaborative, I launched a death and dying conversation group where we could talk about something that is rarely mentioned in polite society. These conversations are helping me to clarify some of the unstated assumptions and unexamined issues lurking in so much of what we talk about when we talk about dying. What is a *difficult* death? It's not just a prolonged and insensible dying hooked up to machines, but a long, drawn-out, steady diminution caused by dementia, stroke, emphysema, cancer. A *good* death, then, is a swift one: a sudden, massive cardiac arrest or an overwhelming stroke seem to be the only natural options, unless the emergency medical technicians get there in time to "help" you. Which in today's medical culture they mostly do, promptly delivering you to the dreaded ICU. A good death has become elusive.

And then there is suicide. Or, as one older couple nicely put it in one of the many articles I have clipped, "ending the dying."

Ending the dying. Talking about this—and starting a death and dying group in order to talk about it—is a public expression of a lifelong concern of mine about being trapped within an incapacitated body. When I was writing fiction in the 1980s and '90s, my best short stories featured a long-married couple facing the devastating illness of one partner, and their painful, fiercely loving agreement to end the dying. These stories were based on situations I had observed: the stroke-induced dysphasia of my mother-in-law's beloved oldest friend. An aunt's emphysema that made her final years a blue-lipped hell. My plots were based on how I imagined my husband, John, and myself handling a similar situation. And suicide—with the reluctant but loving assistance of a beloved partner—seemed like the obvious answer.

Now I am the age of the characters in stories I wrote some twenty and thirty years ago, and things don't look nearly so straightforward. While I still argue that suicide is the only way to maintain control over one's own dying, it is also annoyingly obvious that one must do it *before* the stroke incapacitates, *before* the dementia forecloses the decision, *before* the EMTs arrive with their machines. And boy-oh-boy-oh-boy, just when is that? In ten years, or five, or next week? Unless I commit suicide before I need to, then I risk losing control over my autonomous future. And if I do it before I need to, I lose some of my brief, precious time in the light. Shall I forfeit even one breakfast, one bike ride, one embrace with John, my companion and lover of almost fifty years?

A lifelong atheist, I am both confident and comfortable that there is no afterlife. Unlike the author Julian Barnes, whose book title *Nothing to Be Frightened Of* indicates the void that appalls him, I have no fear of personal extinction. But—and a big *BUT* it is—I have an abiding fear of the loss of control. Of entrusting my physical self to others. Of yielding to the likely loss of all dignity. Someone of my temperament and mindset finds it hard to be a committed activist for *slow medicine* and *natural death.* Sure, I want to see doctors make fewer interventions when the interventions are futile. Sure, I will encourage other people to complete their advance directives so that their preference for nonintervention is documented for the medical team. But really, absent that sudden and massive cardiac arrest, a natural death looks like passive suicide to me—and what I want is assisted suicide. When my body is a burden, I want help snapping the venetian blinds of my life shut with a quick, resounding *clack.*

Well, good luck with that! Doctors may be persuaded to stop prolonging the dying, but in very few places in the United States are they allowed to end the living. What, then? A book that I keep on my bedside table suggests the plastic bag route. Some sleeping pills, a couple of shots of vodka, and a plastic bag, perhaps pulled on over a base-ball cap so that the plastic doesn't bother your nose too much while you suffocate. Inflating the bag with helium is suggested as a possibility. Helium is sold at party stores, so unlike fentanyl or high-grade heroin, you don't need to step across town into the drug culture to get some assistance. When I reviewed the helium option with John, I was reduced to tears of laughter at the thought of my final good-byes conducted in an Alvin the Chip-munk voice. I'd certainly die laughing.

But wait. Suppose John is not there for me to say a giggling good-bye to in my helium-induced squeak. Although I am fully aware of all the sta-tistics indicating that he is likely to predecease me, all my suicide scenarios are about *him* helping *me*. Never about me assisting him with his suicide. Well, it is so clearly unthinkable that I have never thought it.

I have never thought it. And he has never asked it.

I suddenly realize now that I have been request-ing that he agree to something I, in my turn, would be brokenhearted to promise. What? *Not* care for him in his decline, whatever shape that takes? Not bend over him, feed him, wipe him, cherish him?

Am I breaking his heart every time I review my plan to commit suicide (with his help) before my fate is out of my hands? Oh, how selfish of me to deny him what I myself would be unwilling to give up! How forbearing of him not to point out my self-ishness! Or, has he all along known and kept quiet about something that I am just now tumbling to?

So: I consider the lens of autonomy and the lens of love. If I look through the latter, I see that because I love and am beloved, I will probably forego my quick and easy death and accept instead a natural death—comfort care and minimal medical intervention. And then this collateral realization: because John is likely to die before me, the person caring for me on the last days of my journey—moistening my lips, wiping my bottom—is likely to be one of my sons or some paid caretaker. Am I at peace with this? Not really. But I am ever so gradually, ever so grudgingly beginning to accept that whatever happens, it is likely to be out of my hands.

In my poetry class, Lyn had another stroke and died. Her partner, Edith, is back in class, her cancer in remission. Carl turned ninety-three. Natalie has a walker. Dan's Parkinson's has gotten worse and he has stopped attending. But not one, not one has committed suicide. My death and dying group has decided to schedule two more meetings and then disband. We have educated ourselves about the high-tech medical culture and learned how intentional we must be in making consequential medical decisions. We have talked about dying and brought death out of the closet. Our youngest member is seventy, our oldest eighty-nine. Not one, not one has committed suicide.

There is much that is out of my hands, and my hands are slowly coming unclenched.

Time Travel

MARTIN TEITEL

As we get older, many of us find ourselves more and more "acquainted with grief." If the author of that phrase, the prophet Isaiah, were alive today, he might well have added our acquaintance with Kübler-Ross, living wills, and Medicare Part B. Given all those considerations, it's easy to lose track of the sometimes deep changes that occur when we live through close encounters with the end of a lifetime.

In recent years I've used time travel to better understand how acquaintance with death has transformed me. Unlike science fiction, my time travel uses no exotic contraptions. Just the placing of my toe in a particular spot.

I live in a small village, near where two rivers join. For years I've walked my dogs every day to the place where the waters of the two rivers boil together. While the pups sniff around, I look back up the river toward the spot where my little house sits. In the past, I knew that if she was awake, my dying wife was looking out over the same lovely vista. Gradually I began trying to imagine walking the dogs on an unknown but inevitable day, looking at the marshy confluence without that gaze accompanying me from within my house.

Tied in a knot of grief and rage and deep bafflement, I tried to imagine who that future man would be, what he would be feeling. One day, as I paused in the early morning light, I put my foot down on a spot in the road where I knew I had been thinking the same thought at the same time the day before. It became a habit, when I reached that place in the road, to try to imagine the person on the other side of an inexorable dark line: a future me without my wife. A world without the center of my world.

How would life look to that future man? How would he manage to place his feet one ahead of the other, and how would he be changed by his looming acquaintance with death? Staring over the marsh formed where the rivers converge, I tried to imagine a future when the cars of hospice people crowding the driveway were gone, the rented hospital bed had been returned, and the unimaginable had happened. Who would I be without her?

Now, years later, I leash up the dogs and we head out on the route we all know in our bones. Some days, I carefully place my foot onto the spot on the pavement by the bridge and stare out over the water back toward my empty house, reaching back through time to that desolate, disoriented man. I imagine myself patting his shoulder as I recall his overwhelming burden. Gradually I've been using that one place in the road to reflect on my transformation by grief.

The previous me by the bridge, stretching his imagination outward into the future, had no idea how the profound loss would feel, nor could he. One thing I tell him, on chilly mornings standing near the bridge when I travel back to those bleak days, is that my encounter with overwhelming loss reshaped my engagement with my own looming demise. In the same place on the road, I also cast myself into the future when there is no old man pacing across the bridge. First—the world without her. Then—the world without me.

What I find, looking into the future, is unexpected. My anticipation of my own death is becoming transformed. Staring out over the marsh into the wind heading toward me, the temperature of my death has changed. I used to picture death as something cold, rigid, and brittle. Somehow, for the future me, death is cradled in warmth: not an abandonment of myself by life but rather a folding inward, a consolidation that feels dense, and secure.

I'm in no hurry to leave this life. As my wife used to say, I have all eternity to be dead. I love pulling on my clothes every morning while the dogs dance around in anticipation of that day's journey into time. But when I do think about myself at my ending, I picture merging more than crumbling; it's a cozy, almost snug feeling. When I turn my mental attention from the future me to that previous grieving guy on the bridge, I can sometimes imagine my wife floating into the warmth and security of her own ending, instead of an icy plunge into dissolution. It turns out that time travel works—I can change the past.

Another result of my time travel is the shrinking of my striving. I spent my career, and in many respects my life, campaigning to get things done. I kept lists of things to do; sometimes I had lists of lists. I secretly reveled in being admonished to take it easy, watch out for burnout, smell the roses. I was in love with verbs, reports listing my accomplishments, and measurements of my progress. As a result, I got a lot done, and actually, I don't regret what my hard work produced.

I used to think the opposite of striving was sloth, lethargy, and inertia. Looking back through time hasn't reversed striving. But I've opened my hand and let much of it fall to the ground. After a lifetime of being infatuated with verbs, I discovered adjectives and the nouns they beautify. The release from striving hasn't meant abandoning getting things done. Instead, what I do every day is liberated from the tyranny of outcomes. After reflexively setting goals for everything I undertook, now I can plunge into actions without a defined end.

These changes are a great gift from that dismayed man years ago, whom I still sometimes visit on my walks. Back then, as my wife lay dying, I stopped setting goals when the only possible result was catastrophe—and I couldn't plan for the unknowable. Left with little choice, I began to relinquish my striving. Standing in that place where the rivers come together, I know that back then I wasn't ignorant of the real meaning of losing the love of my life. But her terrible demise accomplished no objective and achieved no goal. My skills at campaigning and crusading were worthless.

Instead of goals and objectives, my peering into the past has revealed life-altering loss, profound grief, intense loneliness. Striving is great for getting things done, and I still make lists to get through my daily chores. But the core lesson from the man back then near the bridge is that my task right now isn't to accomplish the rest of my life. Conclusions and ramifications have lost their clout: my own culmination will happen without me knowing it. Relinquishing framing life as a project, in favor of life as nothing beyond a morning walk at sunrise has slowly freed me from carrying around my own fear of death in daily life. That fellow near the bridge years ago has removed a substantial burden, for which I thank him.

And finally, when I embrace the desolate man from years back, and he in turn helps release me from striving through my life, I'm awash in thankfulness. A life pinned to goals and measurements of success inevitably leads to loss and failure. And marching through life accumulating accomplishments is circular, because striving has only one child: more striving. As I've relinquished my zeal for goal setting and checking off fleeting successes from my life lists, the color of the light illuminating my days has changed from the cold blue of appraisal to a rose glow of appreciation and peacefulness. Nowadays I don't feel successful as often as I feel lucky.

Crunching along in the morning I set my foot down in the familiar spot. It's the same foot and the same dogs. The same me. Looking back, I can extend my thanks to the man years ago who endured what he had to, and gave me the powerful gift of a serene day, today. Turning my time-traveling gaze toward the future, I look out over the marsh. I don't see myself. Instead, I see a flock of gulls winging up into the air, into the rising sun.

The Path

MARK BELLETINI

My knees ache.

So I go to see Dr. Rich. He asks me, "You're sixty-five, right?" I nod, and he then says, "Mark, this is a pretty common problem for men of your age." He assured me I was still a long way from any surgical fixes.

Looking back on that day, I find that what really surprised me was not the pain as much as the news that I even *had* knees! I'd never noticed them before. I used to bound up and down steps unconsciously, without any pain, and with an energy that surprised many peers, even when I was in my fifties.

Now I climb stairs slower, more deliberately, and often in pain. One step at a time. Both feet on each step, and then again. The skinny fifteen-year-old who could painlessly bend his knees and tie his legs in yogic knots (surely the only Catholic schoolboy in Detroit to be doing so in 1964) no longer exists. Except in my own memories.

And aging has brought a flood more of those, too. *Tidal waves* of memories.

I walk down High Street in Columbus, Ohio, on a warm summer day, and suddenly the sunlit gables of shops along Telegraph Avenue in Oakland, California, my former home, flash into view right before my eyes.

Or I might see that remarkably bright street in Punta Arenas, a sabbatical retreat in southernmost Chile, the wind blowing hard enough to make me think it would bend the rays of the midnight sun.

I sit in my office at the Unitarian Universalist Church in Columbus, and suddenly I sense the floral sweetness of the grapefruit blossoms wafting into my former office in Hayward, California. Or when I hear the voice of Marian, our office manager in Columbus, I hear the comforting voice of Phyllis, my incredible secretary in Hayward for twelve years, and whose remains have been buried for even more years than that.

I sit on my red sofa in my loft on Rich Street in Columbus, and suddenly I *see* plenty of red. I see the red buildings in San Miguel de Allende, Mexico, where I visited my friend Farley; or the brick-red trousers I used to wear when I was in seminary in Berkeley; or the sacramental crimson apple my friend Stephen shared with me not long after he told me that he knew he was going to die.

The memories swamp me sometimes. They almost drown me. Strangely, most of them seem to be images without any obvious significance: a hickory branch reflected in the dark green Osage River when Flip and I inner-tubed down the shallow waters; a sweep of sunlight on cornices arching over a street William and I strolled down in San Antonio; the refreshing taste of sour grass I used to nibble on in the yard of the day care center where I worked in Berkeley; the dun glint on the old silver Unitarian communion cup on my shelf that Bernie Loomer gave me before he died; the chartreuse quality of the light in the kitchen where Richard first introduced me to red-headed Doug; the black Greek lettering on Finkbone's rainbow-hued tattoo; the gray watercolor drip falling through the orange tiger lily Kevin just painted. Thousands of sensual memories have been erupting in me without ceasing since I turned sixty. My mind flickers all the time between past and present.

Amid these inconsequential images, *are* memories of great import too: the faces and even scents of those I loved in my life, like my grandparents, or the five great loves of my romantic life; my steady friendships of many decades or even the brief flashing friendships that never took permanent root. And then there is the long, somber procession of losses: to AIDS in the late 1980s and early '90s especially, to drugs and alcohol, or to suicide more recently. As I get older, the so-called normal losses: less dramatic but still life-bending deaths of those who have lived many, many decades and whom I have loved as long.

All of these aspects of aging are starting to reveal themselves as a remarkable path, a well-illuminated path of spiritual exercise. *Spiritual* defined in the only way that really centers me and makes sense to me—namely, the practice of constantly shedding our illusions, as psychologist David Richo often puts it.

Illusions. A pretty sinewy word, I'd say. Unequivocal.

Richo outlines some of the illusions a spiritual practice might help me slowly relinquish: The illusion that my unique life, by the very reality of its uniqueness, is utterly separate from others, an indivisible unity, and that I can relate to others only if they are like me, mirroring my own ego. The illusion that someone, or something, can fulfill all my needs and quench my longing once and for all. The illusion that I need to be in control of everything so as not to be overwhelmed by feelings, especially those that clog the heart when approval ebbs, shame tightens, or our plans and hopes—often unconscious—are dashed. And finally, the illusion that I am *entitled* to be totally protected from loss and harm as if I were still a babe in loving arms. (And not everyone received even that when they were born.)

And so, just as I was surprised that I even *have* knees, I find I am more and more astonished that at age sixty-five *I* have not taken up a spiritual practice; rather, it has taken up me. The spiritual path of growing older, illuminated by ten thousand memories, seems fused to my days. As I move through my mid-sixties, and note the inexorable trail of losses behind me, I find I am giving up expecting anyone or anything to protect me from these losses, losses that life simply is heir to by being itself. I still mourn, mind you, as deeply as I have ever grieved. But I no longer expect anyone to secure me against such loss, or even the pace of constant change and rapid passage of the years.

As my health shifts with increasing years and I experience changes in my short-term memory, my focus, and my energy, I feel less and less entitled to live a life without distress or confusion. (Although I have to admit that this has been more of a gradual uphill climb, not quite the clutching hand suddenly opening to relinquish all entitlement, since I have known more than my share of privilege.)

As the memories, both significant and insignificant, rush through me, I find I no longer spend as much time as I once did imagining *the one* who will come sweep me up into some permanent and final romance, my sixth great love that will thrive at least up to the edge of forever, if not beyond. No one has that power, and I say that even if I *were* to marry one day.

Because, mind you, I still have the capacity to fall in love. I've never been one to close off in bitterness, even before I accepted the reality of aging. Indeed, despite a broken heart, my heart seems to remain remarkably open for reasons I don't entirely understand. But I am finally moving away from fairytale land. As I age, I find that I don't have to spend all my time with people who are a lot more like me than not, people who mirror my ego. Somewhat to my surprise, I find that people who are wildly different from me are more welcome in my life.

Still, I am not weeding out *all* my illusions. For example, a number of years ago I asked my mother a question about age. She was, I seem to remember, the same age I am now, and I was born when she was twenty-three. I said to her, "Ma, I can't ask it any better than this, and if you don't understand, it's certainly okay, because it's an odd question, but, uh, how old are you really, on the inside, I mean?"

She looked up at me, raised an eyebrow, then got a little smile on her face and said, "I know exactly what you are asking. I'm twenty-seven on the inside."

"So am I," I said, somewhat surprised we were the same age on the inside. "But Ma, how do you deal with it when you look in the mirror and see that you are not *really* twenty-seven anymore?"

She laughed and said, "I don't look in the mirror."

And that is one of my favorite memories among them all.

So I find myself at age sixty-five acting in ways others sometimes find a bit perplexing. Many of my friends in Columbus are young, in their thirties and even their twenties. I have long attended a potluck on Sunday evenings where I am basically two to three times older than everyone else there. It's a wonderful time filled with laughter and camaraderie. I am not, God help me, a mentor. I am one of the gang. I listen as they struggle with the issues many people that age struggle with, gay or not. Sometimes I comment, mostly I don't. I do share a story now and then, if I think it really blesses the conversation, but I do so less and less. I marvel at their technical skill with smartphones, still often something of a struggle for me, although I am learning. They are energetic, alive, and yes, they allow me to not look in the mirror.

Then I get up to go, and my knees ache. Damn.

My adopted son, Tony, is thirty this year. He too is alive in ways that flirt with my illusion that I really am around his age. We go out together when he is in town. It's less the old man taking him out to dinner and more that we are two companions exploring the world together. He tells me one day when I mention the effects of age on me, "Oh, don't worry, Babbo (Italian for Dad), I'll take care of you when you can't care for yourself anymore."

I weep when he says that, because, well, he says it, for one. But I also find myself fostering the illusion that those days are a long way off, so far off in the misted future that I can't really imagine them. They elude me. I try not to think I will undergo the two decades of Alzheimer's disease that shrouded my grandmother Anna. ("They'll have a cure by then, right?") And this, despite the age spots on my arms, the heart problem and prostate enlargement I medicate, the splintering short-term memory often associated with my years, and those damn fool knees.

Yet the illusion that Tony and I are almost the same age *is* permeable. The aspects of aging involving so much grief for loved ones in my life have seen to that. Tony and I actually have talked about my death quite openly. I have to confess that sometimes it's my head talking to his heart when we do, because it's hardly easy; but we do talk.

However, because of his deep maturity of soul and reliably amazing heart, when it comes time for what the psalmist calls "deep calling unto deep," I know we will flow into that conversation with an even richer version of the wondrous love that has sustained us so beautifully all these years.

As I have moved through my sixties, I sometimes have said that aging is compulsory Buddhism. I am convinced Siddhartha Gautama, the Buddha, was right: Everything flows and changes, and never stays. Even though aging has always invited my perpetual letting go, I have not lost myself completely in that tidal wave of memories. Nor have I relinquished all images of my limited future to the younger generation quite yet. I find I am still open to new and unexpected things, right around the next corner. I see my coming decades (should I be so fortunate as to live a long life like my grandparents) just as likely to be filled with possibilities as with limits; I see open doors as well as locked gates.

It's a path, remember, this aging, a path of spiritual exercises. It's not an inn, a terminal, a destination, or even a line to cross by a certain year so that you can then say, "Okay, now I am really old." My aching knees may not like the path metaphor. Nevertheless, the spiritual path of aging unfolds itself before me every day and helps me shed more and more illusions of attachment, control, and self-doting, which have marked earlier eras in my life.

And as I confessed, I have a few illusions I may hold on to a bit longer.

But the aging process has clearly become for me a shimmering and unexpected version of more famous spiritual paths: meditation, contemplative prayer, silent retreats, the disciplines of art, yoga, or tai chi.

The only difference?

I didn't choose it.

It chose me.

About the Contributors

Mark Belletini has been senior minister of the First Unitarian Universalist Church of Columbus, Ohio, for the last seventeen years. He previously served congregations in California over his nearly forty years in ministry. His son Tony, his sister, and his friends ground his life in love.

Burton D. Carley has served as minister of the First Unitarian Church of Memphis, Tennessee, "The Church of the River," for thirty-one years. He also served for ten years on the Board of Trustees of the Unitarian Universalist Association (UUA).

John Cummins is minister emeritus of the First Universalist Church of Minneapolis, which he served from 1963 to 1986. He has served two terms as president of the United Nations Association of

Minnesota and attended the White House Conference on International Cooperation at the invitation of President Johnson. In 1991, together with his wife, Drusilla, he received the UUA's Distinguished Service Award.

Denise "Denny" Taft Davidoff currently serves as the senior consultant for development and alumni affairs at Meadville Lombard Theological School. Previously, she has served with the Unitarian Universalist Women's Federation, the General Assembly Planning Committee, the UUA Board of Trustees, and as the moderator of the UUA from 1993 to 2001. She is an active member of The Unitarian Church in Westport, Connecticut.

Richard S. Gilbert, a born Universalist, retired after more than fifty years in Unitarian Universalist ministry. He serves as the president of the Unitarian Universalist Retired Ministers and Partners Association. He lives with his wife in Rochester, New York, where he enjoys spending time with their children and grandchildren.

Maureen Killoran came to the US from Canada nearly three decades ago. Since then she has served Unitarian Universalist congregations in eight states in parish, community, and interim ministry. She and her husband, Peter Hyatt, share ten grandchildren. She is eager for the new adventures retirement will bring.

Judith Meyer is minister emerita of the Unitarian Universalist Community Church of Santa Monica, California. She now lives in Knoxville, Tennessee, with her husband, David Denton, and their elderly Shiba Inu, Aki, who provides daily insight into growing old with dignity and attitude.

Peter Morales is the president of the UUA. Before his election in 2009, he served as minister at Jefferson Unitarian in Golden, Colorado. Before entering the ministry he worked in community journalism. He and his wife, Phyllis, have been married since 1967. They have two children, Miguel and Marcela.

Phyllis B. O'Connell has been a parish minister for twenty-five years. Newly retired, she welcomes and enjoys opportunities to guest preach and lead adult education programs on aging and retirement for Boston-area churches. Retirement has given her time to do all her favorite things, including longer Skype calls with her twenty-two-month-old grandson in faraway Dubai.

Jane Ranney Rzepka spent her adult life happily as a Unitarian Universalist minister. By now the kids have launched, the hair is gray, and the stories overflow. She and her husband, Chuck, live in Lexington, Massachusetts, where she is living out every embarrassing cliché related to retirement.

Tom Schade served as minister at the First Unitarian Church of Worcester, Massachusetts, from 1999 until 2012, when he followed his wife, Sue, to Ann Arbor, Michigan. He serves on the CENTER committee of the Unitarian Universalist Ministers Association and blogs as "The Lively Tradition." He is father to two daughters, grandfather to three, and the spiritual director to two little dogs.

Carl Scovel grew up in war-torn China as the son of medical missionaries. During seminary he cared for elderly patients in a hospital. He served as minister to The First Parish of Sudbury, Massachusetts, and King's Chapel in Boston. Married for fifty-six years, he and his wife have three married offspring and seven grandchildren.

William Sinkford currently serves as senior minister of the First Unitarian Church of Portland, Oregon. From 2001 to 2009, he served as president of the UUA, the first person of color to hold that position.

Gary E. Smith is minister emeritus of the First Parish in Concord, Massachusetts, and has retired to Belmont, Massachusetts, where he continues to serve the UUA. He and his wife, Elizabeth, have two children and four grandchildren, life's great joy.

Lynn Thomas Strauss was ordained in 1990 and served as the minister to Unitarian Universalist congregations in Knoxville, Tennessee; Bethesda, Maryland; and Rockville, Maryland. Previously, she taught elementary school and was a mental health counselor. She has raised four children.

Martin Teitel is retired after nearly fifty years working for non-profits and foundations in the United States and abroad. He is the author of five books and numerous articles. He has three children and one grandchild. He is a member of the Unitarian Universalist Church of Brunswick, Maine.

Kate Tucker is minister emerita at First Universalist Church of Minneapolis, where she served as associate minister from 1997 until 2012. Her Universalism has been shaped by the farm fields of central Illinois, the deserts of Arizona, and the Quaker tradition. She lives in St. Paul, Minnesota.

Patricia Tummino is minister emerita of the First Unitarian Universalist Society of Middleboro, Massachusetts, where she served for twelve years before retiring in 2010. She and her husband, Larry, live in Middleboro, where they raised their three children. They have one very fabulous grandson.

Susan Weston lives in Providence, Rhode Island, with her husband, John Weston. Her published works include an introduction to the poet Wallace Stevens, a novel, short fiction, poetry, and essays. She takes great joy in her garden, her two scientist sons and their four children, and the long leisurely mornings afforded by retirement.